AUDACIOUS
Creativity

Also by Stephanie Gunning

Books

The American Institute of Homeopathy Handbook for Parents (with Edward Shalts)
Creating Home Sanctuaries with Feng Shui (with Shawne Mitchell)
Creating Your Birth Plan (with Marsden Wagner)
Easy Homeopathy (with Edward Shalts)
Exploring Feng Shui (with Shawne Mitchell)
Thriving After Breast Cancer (with Sherry Lebed Davis)
Total Renewal (with Frank Lipman)
Whiff (with C. Russell Brumfield and James Goldney)
Will Power (with John Basil)

Audio Programs

Partner with Your Publisher
Planning Kick-Ass Book Events (with Carol Hoenig)
Seven Quick & Easy Steps to Write AND Sell Your First Book Proposal
Social Media for Authors (with Marty Fahncke)
Nine Steps to Heaven (with Kayhan Ghodsi)

AUDACIOUS Creativity

30 Ways to Liberate Your Soulful Creative Energy—and How It Can Transform Your Life

STEPHANIE GUNNING

Creative Blast Press
New York, NY

First published by CREATIVE BLAST PRESS,
a division of Stephanie Gunning Enterprises LLC.
33 West 63rd Street, Suite 3C
New York, NY 10023

Copyright © 2008 by Stephanie Gunning.
The copyright of each selection in this book is the property of the respective author.
All rights reserved.

For information about special discounts for bulk purchases, please contact:
sales@stephaniegunning.com

Cover design by Cheryl Harrison

Without limiting the rights under copyright above, no part of this material may be reproduced, stored in or introduced into a retrieval system, or transmitted, in any form, or by any means (electronic, mechanical photocopying, or recording, or otherwise) without the prior written permission of both the copyright owner and the above publisher of the book.

ISBN-10: 0-615-23488-7
ISBN-13: 978-0-615-23488-5

For my mom, Valerie Gunning, and my dad, James Gunning, who made it possible for me to explore words, music, and dance at an early age and have encouraged me since then to create a good life and a better world

*"If I create from the heart, nearly everything works;
if from the head, almost nothing."*
—Marc Chagall (1887–1985),
Russian painter

"Inherently, each one of us has the substance within to achieve whatever our goals and dreams define."
—Mark Twain (1835–1910),
American novelist

Contents

Acknowledgments   i
Introduction   iii

Surprise Me, *Stephanie Gunning*   3
Solomon's Story, *David Ellzey*   7
The Spiritual Practice of Creativity,
   Reverend Allan Lokos   13
Chariot of Fire, Field of Grace,
   Paulette Callen   25
The Creative Voice—A Bridge Between the Tangible
   and the Intangible, *Katherine Scott*   29
Echoivity, *Martine Bellen*   40
We Make It All Up Anyway . . . Might as Well
   Make It Up Good! *Laura Duksta*   45
How "Positive" Is Positive Thinking?
   Robert and Michelle Colt   53
Soul Currency—Invest Your Inner Wealth,
   Ernest D. Chu   59
The Wizard Within, *C. Russell Brumfield*   71
The Language of a Free Soul,
   Reverend Susanna Weiss   83
Mapping Dreams, Creating Reality,
   Paige Stapleton   93
Ten Guaranteed Ways to Stifle Creativity,
   Kim Marcille   102

Are You Pregnant? Five Ways to Get That Labor Over Quickly and Give Birth to Your Possibilities, *Sandy Grason* 108
Want to Write Like Mozart? *Janet Conner* 116
Inspiration, Desperation, and Curiosity Beget Creativity, *Carol Hoenig* 120
Creativity Rising, *Maria Yraceburu* 125
Creating Your Ideal Life? It's Always Up to You, *Howard Falco* 131
Building a Better Generation, *Rebecca Linder Hintze* 141
Creative Decision-making, *John Darrouzet* 146
Manifesting a Healthy Life, *Kathi Handt and Jay Handt, D.C.* 156
Be and Grow Rich, *Richard Aronow* 165
Butterflies in Winter, *Ann Moller* 175
The Write Muse-IC, *Laura Faeth* 180
Power, Freedom, and Grace, *Mary Jane Mahan* 189
The Soul and Creativity, *Meg Haworth, Ph.D.* 200
Five Creative Benefits of the Conscious Use of Voice and Music, *Eliana Gilad* 210
Creativity Is Life, *Elaine Springer* 217
Beauty and Fear, *Dr. Beatrice Kraemer* 221
For the Love of It, *Jeff Fasano* 226

Contributors 236
About the Editor 270

Acknowledgements

This book was the collective effort of many people who were inspired by the vision of a book on the power of personal creative expression.

I wish to thank all of the contributors who took time out of their work schedules and very busy lives to share their personal and professional wisdom about what makes us creative, how it happens, and what the effects of creativity are on our lives and in service to the world.

Special thanks to Cheryl Harrison of Eden Isle Publishing for her original cover design, which so perfectly captures the playful spirit of this project. I also appreciate the professionalism of Allison Brown and the Book Surge team. Thanks to Sara Whitcomb for casting her eagle eye on the proofs, and also to Tracey D'Aviero and Kayhan Ghodsi for their help with my interior design.

My love and gratitude extends to my publishing clients, coauthors, and the students in my courses for inspiring me to locate my authorial voice, and giving me the avenues to share my expertise.

Thank you, Michel Zadi.

"The day came when the risk to remain in a tight bud was more painful than the risk it took to bloom."
—*Anais Nin (1903–1977),
French novelist*

"To create one's world in any of the arts takes courage."
—*Georgia O'Keefe (1887–1986),
American painter*

Introduction

Several months ago, during a daily meditation, a clear insight told me to gather the wisdom of the authors, speakers, workshop leaders, expert trainers, life coaches, healers, and consultants who are my colleagues, clients, and friends—in other words, the most highly creative, enthusiastic, and successful people I know—and deliver it to you. This collection, *Audacious Creativity*, is the result.

The same day I received my hit of inspiration I began reaching out, seeking contributors who would share what they have discovered about the creative impulse and its important role in every aspect of our lives from our careers and hobbies to our relationships, health and wellness, spirituality, finances, joy, fulfillment, and self-expression. I wanted to collect the most valuable knowledge on being a human being in a complex world. Then it took several months of invitation, coaxing, discussion, and editorial collaboration to produce the 30 essays you're holding in your hands. All this was done while running a publishing consultation business, Stephanie Gunning Enterprises.

Honestly, I feel proud of this accomplishment. It's been a different experience for me to be the publisher of a volume such as this. Years ago I worked alongside Arielle Ford on four Hot Chocolate for the Mystical Soul anthologies, so the scope of this undertaking wasn't a surprise to me. I've collaboratively written 18 nonfiction books. But it has taken me a number of years to shift from playing a supportive role to taking on leadership. The benefit of steering this project myself was to design it as a vehicle for the philosophy that all people are inherently generative and expressive. This is the guiding vision that fuels my creativity.

In these pages, you're going to meet celebrated authors of books that have touched the lives of hundreds of thousands of people. You'll learn how to make better decisions, design vision boards that help you imagine a fulfilling future, overcome the fear of self-expression, access your inner genius, get into the flow of universal energy, manifest wealth, raise good kids, enjoy optimal health, and lead an energized lifestyle. Sometimes you'll be moved to tears, and other times to laughter. The contributors are poets, ministers, musicians, healers, psychologists, businesspeople, life and career coaches, shamans, actors, photographers, and dreamers.

The phrase "audacious creativity" comes from the recognition that it takes a good deal of heart and guts to live as a bold and unfettered creator. It's audacious to dream out loud. It's audacious to claim center stage. It's audacious to speak your truth. It's audacious to be original, colorful, and sincere. But isn't it worth it? I certainly think so.

When groups of creative people get together in person there's combustion of life forces, like a volcanic eruption, which is exhilarating to experience. The connection between creators is transformative. It enriches lives—first their own, then others'. Books share this capacity. So it is my genuine hope that sparks of illumination leap forth from this collection and ignite your imagination. The circle will be complete when you feel as if your own creativity has exploded.

> Au·da·cious (aw-**day**-shŭs) *n.* 1. intrepidly daring, adventurous, bold, 2. marked by originality and verve.

AUDACIOUS Creativity

"We should consider every day lost on which we have not danced at least once. And we should call every truth false that was not accompanied by at least one laugh."
—*Friedrich Nietzsche (1844–1900), German philosopher*

Surprise Me

Stephanie Gunning

"It often seems to me that the night is more alive and richly colored than the day."
—Vincent Van Gogh, September 8, 1888

Creativity is a high-energy state where mental sparks are flying and the improbable seems graspable. It is a state of being that feels infinite, because life is infinite and creativity makes us feel alive. Ecstatic explosions occur as the real world of sensual experience collides with the fluid, limnal interior world of memory and imagination. Even the tiniest spark of these creative blasts transforms everything within us because, as they stir up our senses, our hearts are engaged and our minds open. They transform everything around us because we are now emitting an energy stream that catches fire in others. Suddenly we're alive and we know for sure what we're capable of accomplishing.

Predictability is the death of creativity. When I have mastered my activities or a certain subject matter, it seems that all I do is recreate my world in the same form—I have the same conversations, handle the same types of projects, face the usual challenges, and come up with the usual solutions—until my world becomes an irritant and I would do anything to dull my perception of it or push it off me violently. When my writing process has drained or frustrated me, or my mind seems stuck in navigating a Möbius strip of one-sided thoughts that could circle through the same twisted trajectory forever (if I let them), my preferred remedy is to enter connection with my body. Stimulating my senses and ramping up my physical system liberates me from my predictable routines.

Interruption has to take place. The phone must be turned off or ignored; the computer must be put in hibernation. Then I have to either lie flat on the floor on my back breathing and promising my muscles that they're being supported, or shift to a new location. Going to the gym and working out. Taking a walk in the park. Attending a tango lesson. One option is silence and stillness. Another option is activity that contains human companionship. Interruption is abandoning what is going on within my mind and personal space to connect with the reality outside me.

I have found that one of the beauties of being a working creator is that you study your character as you mature and learn yourself well. You don't get fooled as easily as you once would have by your mind's puzzles. Your spiritual and humanitarian toolkit expands. You get more resourceful. In time, you develop specific processes for being a person of the certain character that is uniquely yours. You understand how to move yourself through states of being, how to support yourself to handle change, and how to be successful at being you. It's true for me and as I reflect upon it, I know it's true for many artists.

Upon completion of my last manuscript, I decided to give myself two weeks to reconnect with myself and recover my pure humanity. I decided to follow my natural biorhythms—no alarm clocks in the morning, no planned schedule of tasks during the day, and no major commitments—and allow my instincts to reveal what would be most healing for me. Only by relaxing was I able to perceive the degree of tension in my body. Only by going hiking in the colorful autumn woods was I able to perceive the blandness of my apartment and the familiar containment of my workspace. Only by lying on my couch in the afternoon listening to the floating violin strains of "Siegfried Idyll" by composer Richard Wagner was I able to perceive the tightness of my mind. Would I ever write again? I lacked all desire to produce. Like the reclusive Greta Garbo, I wanted to be left alone.

A close friend invited me to accompany her to an exhibition of Van Gogh's paintings at the Museum of Modern Art one evening. On this occasion, I saw a piece that I had never seen before: *The Starry Night Over the Rhone* (1888). At first glance, the image took my breath away. On the canvas, points of light radiate over a quiet harbor full of sailboats at rest. Their illumination is captured and reflected by the water, which transforms them into wavering lines of light beams in the gentle waves. The scene of the harbor lights burning on the shore mimics the spectacle of the sky above. A few pedestrians stroll by the docks.

The painting is a precursor of the artist's famous *Starry Night* painted one year later. It was the first of its kind, because Van Gogh apparently liked to paint live from nature and the darkness was a challenge that it took him some time to fathom. Unlike the swirling, visibly windy stars of the second painting, in the one that riveted my attention the stars are conceived with heavy golden dollops of paint. The texture is as emotionally penetrating as the color. I could have leapt inside the frame and been transported onto the docks for a spark of genuine feeling was lit in me.

Transported I was, for sure. I could remember summer—not just one, many. The air was warm as I strolled in conversation with two friends on a visit to a small Middle Eastern port town three years before. Lights were reflected from across the bay. We stopped and asked a young man to take our photograph. He refused. Twenty years earlier, I sat on a dock in a harbor of an island in the Cyclades (I forget which) drinking beer and eating a sandwich. Two sailors invited me to dinner in the local *taverna*. I accepted because I was hungry and wanted to practice speaking Greek. These sweet men ended up giving me a lift on their ship carrying cement to the next island. In childhood, my family lived by a large lake during the summer. I loved swimming underwater with my eyes wide open. Eventually I could hold my breath for three full minutes and found it fun to surprise my siblings by mischievously popping up behind them.

As I looked at Van Gogh's painting, I felt nostalgia for those days. I perceived the aesthetic qualities of light and water. I admired the artist's technical skill, and the imagination of the man, now long deceased, who lives on through the products of his imagination. I felt grateful to recognize that someone somewhere at some time has been, is being, or will be affected by illumination cast off by my own creations. I would not have been affected as I was by the art I saw if I had not had the life experiences I've had. Van Gogh reached me because I was reachable. The creativity was not only in his act of creation; it was also a process within me inspired by the stimulation of his visual image.

Now, there are stars in my keyboard for you.

Solomon's Story

David Ellzey

It all began with a small swatch of white greasepaint that I painted on my forehead. As I applied my makeup, as usual, I had no warning of what was to come that day.

For 12 years, in addition to global travels in support of the awakening human spirit, I have traveled the corridors of pediatric care units in hospitals garbed in a white doctor's jacket, clown-suggestive clothing, and sporting a small red nose. As a clown doctor named Dr. Spaghetti, in the Big Apple Circus Clown Care Programs, I perform humorological surgery, applying a few laughs here and there with family and staff to support healing what could be diagnosed as terminal seriousness, or the natural fear and grief that arise in hospitals.

On this particular day, my partner and good friend Kenny Raskin (aka Dr. Mensch) and I prepared our makeup and costumes in the dressing room and then entered the general halls of the hospital on our way up to pediatrics. Chuckles and downright laughter echoed around us as surprised hospital visitors tried to cope with our claims of being the hospital's newest brain surgeons. The elevators are always fun. Being in closed quarters with a clown standing next to you holds lots of possibilities, as mischievous as we are. We entered the pediatric floor and checked in at the nurses' station for special information on the current patients. Then we began our controlled and loving mayhem.

We visited a few rooms and were approaching the next when a nurse came running down the hall and tapped me on the shoulder. "Solomon needs to see you," she said. (Solomon is the name I've given this young special soul in order to protect his identity.) Kenny and I knew Solomon well. A 16-year-old boy, Solomon had cancer. He had been in and out of the hospital for four years receiving chemotherapy and treatment. And he loved us. Normally a teenager might have reservations about being entertained by clowns, but Solomon had an open and loving heart, and a willingness to surrender to laughter and play. We immediately went down the hall to the room, stood at the door, and peered in. Inside there was a sense of darkness, of heaviness.

We entered slowly, assessing the atmosphere and family. Solomon's parents were Hassidic Jews. His dad was tall and had a dark, long, full beard. He stood on one side of the bed. Next to him, Solomon's mom was quietly crying. She wore a traditional scarf wrapped around her head. In the bed lay Solomon, his face pale and with pronounced cheekbones. His eyes were open and staring blankly toward the ceiling. His chest was barely rising and falling. There was a long pause between each breath, and clearly he didn't have much remaining strength.

As we stood at the bottom of the bed, humble visitors, we held a respectful distance, knowing that what was called for here was not our normal fare but a tender reverence for the reality that was emerging before us and the family's clear pain about their impending loss. And yet, real as it all was, I'll be damned if I didn't still see a glimmer in Solomon's eyes, distant as it was. Maybe it was only my wish or my imagination, but it is what we have learned to search for as practitioners of lightness.

Finally, in a low Yiddish voice, Solomon's father broke the silence. "Dr. Spaghetti, Solomon wants you to sing his song." Kenny and I immediately knew what he was referring to. We now had our clear assignment. Solomon loved this song for a special reason. It was the classic children's song "I'm a Little Teapot" but with an added twist learned when I was a kid. The lyrics are, "I'm a little tea pot, short and stout. Here is my handle. Here is my spout. When I get all steamed up, hear me shout . . ." And then I add, with a full throaty voice, "Sock it to my baby, let it all hang out!"

By itself, that might make others in the room smile a bit. But what has always added to the impact of this song is something my partner does that is a rare and surprising skill. I begin singing the song, while slowly and ceremoniously Kenny removes two small flutes from his pockets and prepares them for playing. He can play them both at once, in harmony. But here's the catch, he plays them at the same time—and not from his mouth. As I sing the first verse, he prepares his mouth as if he is about to blow the flutes, raises them slowly toward his lips, then bypasses his mouth and inserts the two flutes straight into his nostrils. After a pause, he starts blowing out his nose to play the song in perfect harmony through the two flutes. Solomon always found this act very amusing.

As I sang and Dr. Mensch played that day, Solomon's mom quietly watched Solomon through gentle tears. "I'm a little tea pot, short and stout. Here is my handle. Here is my spout. When I get all steamed up, hear me shout, sock it to me baby, let it all hang out!"

We are still. The room is still. His mom is still. We all gently observe Solomon. His face remains gaunt and still, not moving. We feel it is time to leave and begin to turn, when almost imperceptibly, his presence, as if coming from far away and garnering all the strength he can muster, begins to lighten up his face. The edges of his mouth—without much fanfare—begin slowly, slowly to rise. Into his eyes a glimmer enters, like an echo, although an important one, of his appreciation. His whole face warms and smiles gently. To myself, I say an emotional, "Yes!" knowing that he has been with us all along.

The light remained in his face for about ten seconds. Then slowly it drained from his face. It disappeared, and his breath stopped briefly. Within a few seconds, his chest rose again and continued its slow pace.

Clearly there was nothing more for us to do. We knew that we had finished our assignment. The father, in his beautiful low and resonant voice, said, "Thank you." We quietly left the room.

In our careers in the hospital we have seen many things. Often we are affected and need to process the impact of what we witness. We continued down the hall, sharing our thoughts about what we had just been through. We knew that Solomon was preparing to exit the stage. He was a bright light, a special young soul, one of those who touch you more than you know until they leave. Indeed, in our relationship with him, he was the one that brought us joy. Clowns, if they are smart, will be witnesses to the laughter they bring, even more than believing they own it or are responsible for it. In this witnessing, we are inspired by its brightness and are touched. Solomon gave us many chances to be moved by his brightness and innocence. We were grateful to have had our time with him.

We walked the halls after visiting his room and about five minutes later in a gentle run, Solomon's nurse caught up to us and stood before us teary-eyed.

I asked, "Solomon?"

With a gentle nod, she replied, "Yes."

In such a moment it is always strange, because we search for something else to share, to say about it all. Yet, there was not much to say. We all loved Solomon. With mutual appreciation, she mustered a soft smile, then turned and walked away.

Once more Kenny and I faced the fact that we have the honor of being with families at wonderful moments both throughout their lives and at the end of life. Solomon's life changed ours before he left. In the context of creativity, why is this story relevant? I tell it for two reasons. First, I forget, so often, how much impact I have on others' lives. I live my life and do what I choose to do, in this case doing what I love as Dr. Spaghetti. It clearly affects other people, but rarely do I get to see or experience the depth. I'm reminded over and over that the amount of impact each of us has is larger than we can ever know.

The second reason for telling this story is that the impact of our creativity is larger and deeper when we are doing something that we love that's an authentic expression of who we are. I have led seminars across the world on topics of quieting the mind and finding happiness, and I love facilitating such events—and I am fed emotionally just as much by being a clown doctor. Somehow or other, in my simply doing what I love, a young boy named Solomon wanted my presence moments before he died. Doing what you love and being creative from your heart and passion can surprise you in its impact.

For me, I must add that Solomon taught me something else I find profound. He dared to ask for what he truly wanted before he died. How many of us are holding back our own permission to do, say, live, or ask for something that our heart desires? The body will end. This is guaranteed. So what are we waiting for? Solomon showed me how to ask for and aim to have, experience, and be what I love while I still can.

Creativity blossoms when we are expressing: writing, painting, or designing from play and joy, or from passion deep inside us. This gives our creativity legs. Otherwise, we resist it, because it is not ours. And we become stuck, as if in mud. Creativity requires that you learn to listen to what really moves you, hear it, and live from that truth. This is a new skill for many of us, yet essential to our being fulfilled.

I love laughter and respectfully interrupting the seriousness of the atmosphere in a hospital. This brings me joy and seems to invite a response from the world that says, "Yes!" Thus, I am fed and inspired to continue.

To discover how to create from joy and passion is powerful, yet to do so while simultaneously giving yourself permission to have what you really desire in life is to fill the well so full that whatever you create overflows from the richest contentment of being.

Thank you, Solomon.

The Spiritual Practice of Creativity

Reverend Allan Lokos

You and I are a process of continually unfolding events. No matter how much we may like or dislike these events, they will all change and ultimately fade away. Don't be concerned if you have never thought about things that way. We have been living with this constant change—the law of impermanence—from before beginning-less time, and will be beyond endless time. It is this very arising and passing of phenomena that inspires creativity and arouses the desire to know one's spiritual self.

I spent the first 30 years of my adult life in the arts as a professional singer on Broadway and in concert and opera. I also taught singers, produced and directed a number of theatrical productions, and even started an artist management company. In short, I was completely immersed in a creative life. Then, for reasons unknown, this gallivanting agnostic entered a seminary and emerged a few years later as an Interfaith minister. The undeniable relationship between creativity and spirituality became manifest in the newest unfolding of me.

In the aftermath of the events of September 11, 2001, my wife and I founded the Community of Peace and Spirituality in New York City. In the early days we thought we had created an Interfaith organization, which from a limited perspective we had. But as spirit and creativity mingled, what emerged instead was a viable, challenging, and inspiring alternative to the dogmatic and confining approach to religion and spiritual pursuits. In fact, what we founded is not about religion at all, but rather a place for personal spiritual exploration supported by a creative, open-minded community.

From the perspective of 30 years in the creative arts and another ten in active spiritual practice, I believe that true creativity is a spiritual experience and spirituality can inspire our truest creativity. I don't think that can be said of religion. Our religious institutions are dedicated to preserving the sanctity of the original teachings of their faith. Therefore, creativity, originality, and imaginative thinking can be in opposition to religious establishment. Whatever creative thinking comes out of religious circles usually manifests, at best, as a new denomination of an existing form.

However, for those looking to be in touch with their spiritual essence—their true self—those looking for a sense of equanimity in their lives and the experience of inner peace, the creative spirit can enhance and inspire the adventure. It can provide the juice for the journey.

I find myself less and less enamored with philosophies and theories about how to live a meaningful life, and more and more interested in

The Spiritual Practice of Creativity

practices that address living everyday life. In everyday life there is heavy traffic when we're late, the office can be hell, relationships are stressed, colds and viruses take up residence in our bodies, and loved ones get sick and die.

I live in New York City. There are those who say that the pursuit of spiritual matters in this bustling, materialistic "Mecca to the buck" town is especially challenging. Perhaps, but for me it has opened up opportunities to create spiritual practices that I need in order to be the person I want to be—practices that I might not have needed in quieter, more sedate surroundings. I think of these as mini, pocket practices, that I can quickly call upon and use at any time. Some uplift my spirit while others provide a method for dealing with my disappointments, anger, insecurity, reactive patterns, or judgmental tendencies. Others simply bring me more in contact with the person I want to be—my kinder, more compassionate, more generous self.

I practice formal meditation each day, but I also keep these exercises ready for immediate use as needed. They don't require a cushion, sacred space, candles, incense, or a holy attitude, just a desire for a greater sense of inner peace and happiness. I have created these practices based on the teachings of those who have preceded me, and as I share them with you, I encourage you to use your imagination and mold them so that they can best serve you on your journey.

It may seem surprising, but spiritual practice is not about becoming a better person. You are already whole and perfect as you are. Spiritual practice is about becoming present to that perfection.

Mindfulness is the quality that opens the door to awareness of our true selves. We become present to what is happening within us and around us as it is happening. Therefore these practices are intended to help us become more aware of our thoughts, feelings, perceptions, and motivations. In other words, these practices help us gain greater insight into the workings of the mind.

Let's look at each one in turn.

Skillful speech. There is probably no practice that can have a more immediate effect on our lives and on those around us than becoming more aware of our speech. Our words have the power to bring joy or to cause misery, to do great good or terrible harm. Buddhists refer to speaking truthfully, compassionately, usefully, and supportively as the practice of *skillful speech*.

The pillar of skillful speech is to always tell the truth, to refrain from telling even "little white lies." That includes exaggerating or minimizing, and self-aggrandizing. Or we could simply follow tee shirt wisdom that says, "Tell the truth, there'll be less to remember." The most important step in developing skillful speech is to think before speaking. It is called *mindfulness of speech*. Our mini-exercise then is: Stop, breathe, and consider what you are about to say before saying it. It sounds easy enough, but in a heated moment, it is easy to slip. That's why it is called a *practice*. Remember, we can never really take back our words.

Here is a practice that can dramatically change relationships. Determine that, in conversation, you will not respond to the other person until you have left at least a five-second period of silence. This may seem long and awkward at first, but stay with it. The rewards can be great. A variation is to quietly take three complete in-breaths and out-breaths before responding. The other person doesn't know we're doing this, but they do know they're not being interrupted and that will feel good. They may also have the sense that we are considering what they have said—which, by the way, is not a bad practice either.

One of the greatest causes of conflict in the world is when people feel they are not heard. Because the brain is so capable, we often assume we know what the other person is going to say and we jump in and respond before they finish. Instead, try this: Notice if, as the other person is speaking, your mind is already off preparing a response. If so, release your thoughts and practice a deeper level of listening.

A word about teasing: *Don't!* Although teasing usually entails a creative use of words, it is always at someone's expense and it usually hurts more than folks let on. Why not use that same creative energy to fashion a kind and uplifting statement instead? That would be creative spirituality, and a beautiful practice.

I had a counseling client who complained that her husband never listened to her and when he did, he always told her she was wrong. "He's such a jerk," she told me. I suggested that name-calling might not be the most effective way to communicate, that perhaps the next time they had a discussion, she pause for five seconds before speaking and in that time try to get in touch with her feelings. Then, begin sentences with "I feel."

When she returned for her next session, I asked how things were going and she said, "Terrible. I tried your suggestion and it didn't work. I took my time, got in touch with my feelings, and said, 'I feel you're the biggest asshole I ever met.'"

A word of caution: All of the exercises suggested here work best when carried out with at least a smidgeon of wisdom.

Here is an exercise that I find incredibly enlightening. It sounds simple enough, but if you are like me, you may need to be creative to manage this. It is about freeing one's self from the tendency to gossip. Gossip is defined as speaking about someone who is not physically present. It has nothing to do with whether what we say is positive or negative. If the person is not there, it is gossip, and gossip is considered one of the most destructive forms of unskillful speech.

For a specified period of time—let's say seven days—do not speak about anyone who is not physically present with you. That's the whole exercise, short and sweet. But I'll tell you that the first time I did this, I was shocked. Now, I do this exercise twice or thrice a year for a week or two at a time. My voice gets a good rest as I find myself participating in many fewer conversations.

Compassion. The great teachers, philosophers, and spiritual practitioners throughout history have all concluded that the greatest happiness we can experience comes from the development of love and compassion. The more we genuinely care about others, the greater our own happiness. For each of us there are those we find easy to love and those whom we find—let's be honest—*unbearable*. Those are the people who push our buttons, who appear rude, arrogant, or greedy. Yet those are the very people we need if we are to advance spiritually. They force us to awaken our spiritual creativity. They are our practice partners.

To be truly loving and compassionate does not mean to be a doormat. A loving, compassionate person is not weak. Quite the contrary. Compassion motivates us to address injustice; if we need to take action, we do it with compassion and wisdom, not anger or ignorance. We need to consciously practice every day until the truly compassionate person we are is always present. While it may seem like an overwhelming prospect, it actually isn't. We need our pocket practices at our disposal, ready to use at a moment's notice.

Here's one to think about: You are doing the best you can, and so is everyone else, including the guy acting like such a jerk. That can be hard to believe, so spend some time with the concept, because it's true.

When we understand and accept this truth, we become more forgiving of others and ourselves, life becomes lighter, and we become more of a friend to the beings on this planet. Now this doesn't mean that we have to accept things as they are. Where we see we can reduce our own suffering and that of those around us by changing our thoughts, words, and actions, we'll want to do so. But understanding that we, and those around us, are doing our best helps us see with greater clarity, speak and act with more patience, and experience less annoyance and resistance. Understanding that we are all doing our best is not only an accurate view of the world; it is a gentler, more compassionate way of living. Think to yourself often, "I'm doing my best." "He's doing his best."

Generosity. The Buddha placed such strong emphasis on generosity that, as a virtuous practice, he placed it even before morality. From this we can conclude that one cannot even begin to lead a moral life with a heart closed to the needs of others. Unfortunately, most of us are bombarded with an endless barrage of appeals from worthy causes that the joy of giving can metamorphose into what feels like an assault on our very person. City dwellers are approached by unfortunate beings with their hands out on every street corner. Our hearts can harden without our realizing that we have cut ourselves off from our fellow beings.

How can we rekindle the joy of a generous heart in a practical and meaningful way? Sometimes simple creativity can produce highly effective results. Try this: Carry at least five one-dollar bills with you at all times. Do not walk past anyone asking for help. Make eye contact with them and engage in a short conversation. "How are you doing?" is a good starter. Give them a dollar and wish them well.

The specific amount can vary in accordance with your resources but not by judging the recipient's worthiness. This exercise needs to be done in a completely non-judgmental way. It's easy to rationalize that the downtrodden might use your gift for drugs or drink, or that anyone who really wants to can find a job, but let's leave out the suppositions. After all, we don't know. We can never know the whole story. Just practice generosity.

One woman told me that this practice helped her get over her fear of a local homeless man and now she looks forward to her chat with him each day. Another shared with me that giving so freely led her to realize how much she had. While she is not particularly wealthy, she saw that she always had enough to share with others.

If you're too busy to spend a moment with someone down on his luck, perhaps you're too busy.

Equanimity. One of my teachers once said, "Nothing can destroy my peace." My first thought was that if I had been a monk for 60 years, living primarily in a monastery, as had he, I could make that statement, too. But then I realized that it is true for me as well, even in the busy secular world in which I live. So I created a practice of stopping and remembering—remembering that I am the only one who can destroy my peace.

Throughout the day, when it seems as if others are making life difficult, stop and remind yourself that you are the one who determines how you feel about what's going on. You are the one experiencing the words and actions of those around you, and your perceptions are entirely up to you. Realizing that only you can destroy your peace is easy. Remembering not to destroy your peace is *not* always easy. Yet, it can be a bit of mischievous fun breathing calmly as others fuss and fume, and thinking to yourself, "You can't destroy my peace. Only I can do that, and I choose not to do so." You might also silently wish them peace and happiness.

Happiness. A partner exercise to "Only I Can Destroy My Peace" comes from something that the

Vietnamese Buddhist monk Thich Nhat Hanh often asks his students, "Are you sure?" We'd say, "Yes." Then he would ask again, "Are you sure?" Most of us tend to be so sure we are right that we don't even consider the possibility that we might be wrong. (What? Impossible!) So we live all puffed up with our rightness, never knowing the joy of being in harmony with the universe. Peace, joy, and equanimity remain meaningless concepts.

I was in the original Broadway company of *Oliver!* There was a scene at the end of the first act in which Oliver picks the pocket of Mr. Brownlow. The whole cast becomes involved in a wild chase trying to catch the elusive little thief. One night, about two years into the Broadway run, I came zipping across the stage chasing Oliver only to find the entire rest of the cast pulling a prank on me by running in the wrong direction. I tried to act cool and go along with the joke while at the same time thinking that they were not acting very professionally in front of a sold-out Broadway house.

When the curtain came down my colleagues remained on stage looking at me with vague smiles, exactly as I was looking at them. The stage manager approached me tentatively and asked if I was all right, and I assured him that I was. "Well then," he barked, "What the hell were you doing?"

Apparently, in a moment of complete mindlessness, I had left out an entire section of staging resulting in everyone else being in the "wrong place." It took me several days to fully accept that *I* was the one who was in the wrong place. Since then I have often wondered if humanity divides itself naturally into those who, when there is disagreement, immediately assume they are right or, just as reactively, immediately assume they are wrong. Either way, we leave out the process of evaluating the information before us and risk not making wise decisions.

All beings want to be happy. Sometimes it doesn't seem that way, because we can get so caught up in the need to be right, as I was with my fellow actors. The effort that goes into needing to be right undermines our happiness. Over time we learn that even if we *are* right, that kind of rightness never brings lasting happiness. We might gain a moment of satisfaction by proving our point, but even that requires the acknowledgment of others. True happiness and inner peace are quieter and gentler and require nothing from outside our self.

Our happiness is not determined by the conditions in our lives. Our happiness is totally dependent upon our *perception* of those conditions. In fact, our entire experience of life is dependent upon how we view the events in our lives. The optimist thinks this is the best of all possible worlds, the pessimist fears that might be true. The optimist says, "The glass is half full." The pessimist says, "The glass is half empty." The rationalist says, "The glass is twice as big as it has to be."

I think many of us question whether it really is okay to be happy the way the world is today. One could almost feel guilty for being happy. There is so much suffering in the world. Is it really okay to be happy? I was raised to believe we are all sinners. Is it really okay to be happy? I've made mistakes that have hurt people. Is it really okay to be happy?

Yes, we have all made mistakes, and yes, at some point, we may have intentionally said or done things to hurt another, and yes, there is terrible suffering in the world. But here is the important point: There is no situation or condition that can be made better by your unhappiness.

It may be too simplistic to say, "Just be happy." Yet it is also foolish to believe that if you change the external conditions in your life, you will then be happy. No event, condition, or object contains within itself either happiness or unhappiness. We supply the emotional response. We are the source of our happiness. The exercise then is to accept that and live it.

Inner peace, happiness, and equanimity are not permanent states. This work is an ongoing creative process. We have to live peace to be at peace. With every thought, word, and action, we create who we are. With every thought, word, and action, we give to our lives the only meaning it will ever have.

> *"Creative thinking is not a talent;*
> *it is a skill that can be learned."*
> *—Edward de Bono (b. 1933),*
> *British physician, inventor, and consultant*

Chariot of Fire, Field of Grace

Paulette Callen

Spirituality and creativity flow from the same source. While one can argue that consciousness itself is by definition creative and of the spirit, we all know the difference between taking out the trash and writing a sonnet. In the eyes of some Zen master somewhere, perhaps they are the same. For most of us in our everyday reality, they are not.

In the film *Chariots of Fire,* Reverend Eric Liddell (played by Ian Charleson), the Scottish Olympic medal winner, is chided by his sister for running because she says it takes him away from his religious work. He replies that when he runs, he feels God's pleasure. The non-religious may use different words for the feeling of doing something to our fullest capability: inspiration, following your bliss, being in the zone or going with the flow, getting outside yourself or connecting more deeply to your own center, magic. Whatever it's called, it feels right. It uplifts and expands and gives meaning to our lives in ways few other things do. It can also make us profoundly miserable.

For most of us, the magic and misery of creation are inherent to only a few of our endeavors, perhaps only one—something that drew us, and then we were compelled to work hard at. As with spiritual work, creative work needs preparation. It is a rare meditator who gets enlightened the first time she sits on a cushion, just as it is a rare artist who takes brush to canvas or pen to paper and creates a masterpiece without study and practice. Ninety-nine percent perspiration and 1 percent inspiration is no lie. The natural talent, the training, the practice, the technique . . . together these fashion the launch pad. Our chariots won't get far without one.

Once launched, where is it that we go? I believe in Rumi's field, "Out beyond ideas of right doing and wrong doing." Mystics (no matter what faith path they may travel) all seem to end up in the same place: beyond language. In trying to express the inexpressible, they resort to words and metaphors that end up sounding similar: light, flowing rivers, a place of peace passing understanding, samadhi, nirvana. Creative artists and, often, interpretive artists, tap into the same place, because there is only one such place. There is only THAT: a place, or state, greater than the synapses in our individual brains; a field beyond ideas, a field of grace. Is it outside or in? Our Zen master would tell us that there is no difference between the outside and the inside, but we won't discover this until we are there.

But what of the misery? The chariot of fire is an apt image of the artist's inspiration. Before it takes flight, a chariot ride is bumpy. Fire burns. Like mystics and spiritual seekers, few artists are spared their dark night of the soul. A chariot is a small craft. There is usually only room for one. Both mystics and artists, until they reach that heaven, that place of peace, are alone.

The threshold when craft becomes art, when the chariot finally lifts off, that's where the magic is, when the gate opens to the field of grace. An artist must have technique, skill, and talent—and then must forget them all and step forward. Any athlete or actor will tell you this. You do your homework, and then, when you step out on the court or the stage, you forget it and stay in the moment (on the cushion, it's called staying present). If you don't, you might fall on your face. The same is true for creative artists; although some artists, like writers, for example, have an advantage . . . we can go back and revise. As our art and craft couple in the dance of creation, our inspiration and perspiration mingle. Our demons revisit us.

The differences between a spiritual and artistic quest are sharp. While issuing from the same headwaters, the streams often take divergent paths. The mystic seldom seeks recognition. She may get it through the students she attracts, but a true mystic is usually content with and prefers solitude. An artist usually burns for recognition. Part of this desire is the craving of the ego, part of it is due to the need to make a living; but mostly, perhaps, it is the longing to connect. Mystics are often connected by a tradition or lineage and supported by a religious institution, or, as in many Near Eastern and Asian countries, by the general population for whom giving alms is meritorious. No such luck for artists. If they can't sell what they make, they live in poverty or take other work that, at worst, does not suit them and, at best, takes them away from their art. If no one sees or appreciates their art, they often feel half alive.

Another difference between the endeavor of the artist and that of the mystic lies in its fruit. An artist creates the tangible, the material. A spiritual seeker re-creates her self. A refinement of the soul, or the mind stream, or one's portion of the collective consciousness goes with you at the end of your physical life. It is the only thing that does. The material does not. An artist may consider that her art has given her a kind of immortality in the public consciousness, but she must leave it behind. Her labors to refine her art have not necessarily led to her own refinement. Artists can be selfish, childish, and cruel. I wish I had a nickel for every time I have heard a person who has been obnoxious, or just plain nasty, being let off the hook because of her "artistic temperament." It is possible for the two streams to flow in one bed. The 16th-century Spanish mystic St. John of the Cross, for example, wrote poems deemed the greatest lyric poetry in Spanish literature.

At the last, both spirituality and creativity are characterized by faith. By *faith*, I do not mean *belief* in a deity or dogma. (This kind of belief can limit as much as it can inform and enrich a person's spiritual and creative life. Belief is not the same as faith, just as religion is not the same as spirituality.) I mean a faith in oneself as containing seeds of possibility, a faith in a future where these seeds might eventually blossom. In the meditation tradition that I practice, emphasis is placed on NOW: there is no past . . . it is gone; there is no future . . . it doesn't exist . . . it might not happen and we can't live there. All we have is this moment. But the paradox is that—even so—whether on our cushions, or in front of our easels or a blank sheet of paper, we exist right now in a shimmer of possibility, a field of grace that is ripe with the future *and* rests outside of time, and without faith in that possibility, we would not meditate, not create, not do anything. Maybe not even take out the trash.

The Creative Voice—A Bridge Between the Tangible and the Intangible

Katherine Scott

When you stand at a window, do you see the world outside or do you see your reflection? When the sun is shining brightly, the window is transparent and you see the physical world. At night, when the light is behind you, the window becomes a mirror and you see your Self.

As your perception shifts back and forth between the mirror and the window, your creative voice is the bridge between the tangible and the intangible worlds. Your creative voice is how you express that which you create.

Think for a moment about the word creativity. Are you thinking of singers, writers, painters, sculptors, composers, poets? Yes, artists are creative. But so are thinkers, philosophers, speakers, teachers, inventors, marketers, and cooks. One of the most creative people I know finds her outlet in preparing food for friends. It brings her tremendous pleasure, and her dinner table would make a brilliant and beautiful magazine layout. All living beings have a form of creative expression that is uniquely theirs.

Creativity could be defined as the ability to see the extraordinary in the ordinary and the profound in the everyday. It could be the act of taking pieces of an old familiar puzzle and synthesizing them into a startling new vision and then contributing that vision to the world. It could be simply receiving an idea and knowing it's something you want to contribute to your Self.

In this expanded view of creativity, everyone is an artist dancing on the bridge between the visible and invisible worlds.

So come with me now as we begin the dance.

The first step in the dance on the bridge is the initial *"Aha!"* moment. You have the first spark of your idea. It's invigorating. You're aware "something" has happened, but before the words come you can't articulate what it is. Nor do you have any clue how it could happen.

You may not be able to find the words but you aren't going to let that stop you. Oh, no! Shake hands with the thought. Say, *"Thank you for coming,"* and invite it in to talk as if you recognized an old friend.

As you take the first steps of your dance, your inner voice might say something like this: *"I receive inspiration every day. This idea has come to me and I am inspired and excited. I'm wondering where it came from, but I'm also confident I asked for it. Right now the inspiration doesn't have all the details in place. But even though I can't yet put it into words, I'm experiencing a sense of elation and it feels wonderful."*

The Creative Voice

As you learn the next steps, you bring your knowledge and perspective to the idea and you begin to see it take shape. Some of the details start to clarify and your imagination takes flight. Now you begin to choose from a multitude of possibilities.

Have you ever had the experience of telling someone about an exciting idea only to have him or her throw cold water all over it? What if the Wright Brothers or Thomas Edison had listened to those people who said it couldn't be done?

Is this a good time to start talking about it? Or is it a good time to hold the idea in silence and conserve your energy for the actual manifestation? Through careful internal listening, you will receive constant guidance about the choices you're making.

Your inner voice at this stage might sound something like this: *"The idea is getting clearer and clearer. I have a better mental picture and I feel excited about all the possibilities. When I think about this idea, I feel a tingle inside me. Yes, I'm ready to take my inspiration further. I wonder if I should talk to someone about it or if it would be wise to wait until I have the complete picture. No one can express doubts if I keep it to myself for a while. You know, the more I think about the idea, the better I like it."*

When you come to the next stage of creation you bring your actual voice into the dance. The outline of the idea is totally formed. You have the ability to articulate what it is. You're getting better at focusing your creative energy on what you want to happen. Now you must separate the knowable "what" from the unknowable "how."

If you listen only to the "how" voice, your inner monologue might go something like this: *"It's a great idea, but I just can't see how it will happen. I don't really have the time with everything else I'm doing. I won't get any support from my family. They're already complaining I don't spend enough time with them. It could be expensive and I don't have the money. I don't know everything I need to know to make it happen. What was I thinking?"*

Sound familiar?

Nurturing your creative embryos requires vigilance about what thoughts you're expressing. One of the myths about creativity is that there isn't any money in being creative. Another myth is that creative energy needs chaos and disorganization to thrive.

Say no to the myths. The joy of the creative voice is your birthright.

So now focus on the "what" voice for a moment. Stand at your window and, placing one hand on your heart and one hand on your solar plexus, speak these words out loud. Feel the power of them.

"This idea is important to me and the doors are opening. The right people will be there to help me when I need them. I have all the time and money and support in the world. I don't have to know how it will happen."

In summer 2006, I moved from Toronto to Vancouver because I wanted to live by the mountains and the ocean. Before I moved, I went online and found a map of all the neighborhoods in Vancouver. I printed a copy and posted it on my vision board. On it I circled the area I wanted to live and I wrote, "I live here," with an arrow pointing to my desired neighborhood.

Several months before the actual move, I flew to Vancouver for a visit to check things out. For the visit, I was unexpectedly gifted with airline credits and free accommodation in a luxury hotel by the water. During that visit, I saw a friend who lived in an apartment in the precise area I was interested in. Four months later, as I realized it was time to book another flight to come and find a place to live, I heard from the manager of that building who had an apartment to rent. It was the exact layout of my friend's apartment, only several floors higher with an incredible view of the mountains and water. It all unfolded effortlessly in ways I never could have imagined. Instead of telling myself it was impossible, I asked with childlike enthusiasm, "I wonder how that's going to happen?"

When we're totally clear on what we're asking for, the right people show up at the right time; we read the right books or have the right dream. To someone standing on the outside it could look like a miracle or, at the least, extremely good luck. From the inside, it's simply bringing into an observable form something that has already been created through inspiration.

On to the fourth stage. This part of the dance on the bridge is where your vision reaches your heart. Do you have the passion to actually bring it into the physical realm? Do you have a fire in the belly? Is your vision juicy and bubbly? The moment when the fire is lit in your heart is a moment of intense connection and appreciation. The flow of imagination sparks the next right action and the next and the next.

Once again, listen in on the creative voice. *"When I think about this idea, I'm even more excited than the day it first came to me. Already so many things I never could have foreseen have helped me move this vision forward. This is so much fun. It makes my heart sing. Any time this project is not feeling joyful, I have the choice to stop. Any obstacle I face is really there to assist me and will just move me further on the path. No matter what anyone else thinks, I have the fire in my heart to make this idea real in the physical world."*

Two or three years ago I read an intriguing story in a magazine about a man who forged a very successful career in the world of finance. He describes how he woke up one day and realized there was nothing more for him to do in the world of finance that excited him. He decided what he really wanted to do was play his music in the subways of New York City. As he gathered his courage to follow his heart's desire, he realized he had to be centered in himself and not care that 98 percent of the people walking by wouldn't even hear him. He had to have the courage to take this step even though he was risking the ridicule of former colleagues who might see him busking in the subway. He had to let go of other people's opinions of how he was choosing to live his life.

What if you were to view your voice as the intersection point for the power of the mind, the power of the heart, and the power of intuition? Can you sense the creative energy of that?

Power is a word often misunderstood and used interchangeably with the word control, but they're not the same thing. Power is an energy that comes from

The Creative Voice

within and in a very real sense manifests in the visible world through the voice. You instantly recognize someone who has aligned with that inner power. You can feel it. You can hear it. You can sense the quality of leadership.

Everyone has that potential.

Yes, fear will come up from time to time. Fear is simply a resistance to something that hasn't happened yet. It's important to respect that resistance and wait until you are in alignment to receive with an open heart and mind.

When I had a singing studio in Toronto, I learned very quickly how strong the connection was between voice and power. Because the voice is the only instrument where musical sound is produced by the body itself, the potential for transformation when using the voice is vast.

As an example, one young woman came for a consultation and, for the first time, tapped into her creative energy. She was excited and set up a second lesson but then phoned to cancel it. She acknowledged she wasn't ready to fully experience her own power. She impressed me with her awareness of herself, and I wasn't really surprised when she phoned several months later to say she was ready.

When your creative power causes you discomfort it's simply because you care deeply about your project. When you take the time to come into alignment with that creative power, your actions will be a response to an invitation rather than a forceful initiation springing from a desire to control the outcome.

Pay attention to the intention, do what is needed to stoke the fire, be willing to not know everything about the outcome, and the resistance will slip away like a thief in the night.

You may have noticed to this point that your journey has been only in your inner world. Now it's time to bring your creative voice to the outer world. Here is where the particular form or structure of all inspiration begins to materialize.

There are as many different forms as there are beings inhabiting this planet. It could be something so small you could hold it in your hand. It could be as tall as a skyscraper that seems to touch the sky. It could be a health breakthrough that will help many people. The number of atoms and molecules in the form is not important. What's important is how joyfully you continue on the journey and how completely you express your essence to the world through the structure that is unique to your creative voice.

Helpers come along. Miracles happen. A book gives you the perfect idea for taking the next step. A friend's offhand remark leads to the solution you've been searching for.

This stage is also where you decide whether you want to be involved in the entire project. If not, open your arms and dance with those people who light up about the parts you don't want to do. Form a partnership that brings about a juicy, fun experience for everyone.

"As my vision manifests, all kinds of synchronistic events happen, and I draw the right people at the right time. I attract people into my life who are good at and love all those parts of the idea I don't want to do. I have the same excitement and passion now as I did at the beginning. There's a bend in the river, but I

The Creative Voice

know there's a good reason I can't see the whole outcome yet. The light burning inside me is all I need to inspire the right action. I get to express my true essence through my relationship to this particular form. This is my song and I must sing it."

Stop for a moment on your journey and think about the ideas that never make it across the bridge into the outer world. Sometimes it's a clear choice to let it go and sometimes they slip away from us. Everyone has lived through both. But if you have an idea that's still waiting, it's never too late.

A few years ago I was very excited about a concept I had for a CD, and I described it to someone with quite a lot of detail. A few weeks later she told me about an idea she'd had for a CD. As she described it the similarities were unmistakable. I was stunned by the fact that she wasn't even aware it was so similar to mine. How dare she steal my idea and claim it was hers? But finally I realized two people could have exactly the same idea and the end result would be distinctly different based on individual knowledge, vision, and perspective. And, indeed, that is what happened.

If you have the passion and fire, you can always bring an old idea to fruition knowing your creation will be different from someone else's.

Now you are finishing your dance. Step by step, your creative energy and unique voice have taken on a concrete form. Your idea has a presence in the world you see outside the window and now the right people will be drawn to learn from and experience your vision.

This is a moment of vulnerability. What if someone doesn't appreciate your vision? Well, some might not. Nietzsche expressed it well. "Those who were dancing were thought to be insane by those who could not hear the music."

At one point in my own creative development, several different people called me unconventional. At first the thought scared me because it seemed to indicate that I was "different." However, I grew not only to accept it, but also to revel in it.

If you create only for the world through the window, criticism will be devastating and the need for approval never-ending. No one else can give you permission to be who you really are.

Dare to be unique and the courage will rise to allow you to be vulnerable. If others reject your offering, remind yourself that you've brought them a wonderful gift of clarity by showing them something they don't want.

One person expressed her insight into her uniqueness this way: "An idea I had previously experienced only in an abstract form became a tangible and emotional reality. I became aware that no one's voice is greater than or lesser than mine. I understood that in being part of a whole, individuality is not lessened, it is enhanced."

In the movie *Wheel of Time*, a film about the sacred Buddhist ceremony of Kalachakra, some of the pilgrims travel to it by advancing only one step at a time and then prostrating themselves full length. They stand up. They take one more step. And then they fall down full length on the ground again. They travel the entire distance to their destination in this deliberate manner.

From moment to moment you choose your speed and direction. Whatever choices you make, they will bring experiences that allow your Self to emerge. What you gain depends on how deeply you trust the experience.

The journey from the moment of inspiration to manifestation is the hero's journey. By exercising your creative muscle you learn new ways of being and knowing. The more you say, *"Yes, please"* to the creative voice, the more complex and fulfilling your inspiration becomes. Can you imagine our world if everyone daily experienced a sense of oneness with Creation?

Now you have come full circle to the beginning, but the dance isn't over. You have simply returned to the place where the next inspiration is waiting for you. Your ideas want you to birth them, to nurture and express them, to send them out into the world to be seen and appreciated and expanded upon. Your most powerful inspiration is called from somewhere in the universe by those who really want it.

Who is transformed by expressing your creative voice in the world?

You are.

If you can be who you are, if you can show your Self to the world, if you can sing the song that only you can sing, you will know hope, you will know joy, and the change in the world will be you.

Echoivity

Martine Bellen

"In the beginning God created Heaven and Earth."

Now . . . look out your window. Turn on your computer. All THIS has been created. See what God started.

As a life form, life force, we are obsessed with creation—at least it appears we are. How often do you run into someone who says, "I don't have a book in me"? I imagine not too often. We make too many babies, buildings, businesses, and, yes, too many books. In the beginning, God created . . . and, then, we took over. Or did we?

I often wonder if our aim is to create anew or if we obsessively and joyously desire to add our voices to the already reverberating echo. Echolalia is a "normal" phase in childhood development, a phase we're supposed to have grown out of. I tend, though, to believe that we never completely let go of the creature comfort that repetition affords us and that, although our relationship to repetition becomes less obvious as we develop, it never severs. Repetition is an innate pedagogical tool to which we naturally gravitate, and it's as pleasurable as the powdery scent of a baby blanket on a sunny spring day. That said, I would conjecture that we, in our own private ways, continually repeat the stories of our species and our youth. Our repetitive tendency is referred to as "forming patterns" in the rhetoric of psychology (we often tirelessly visit shrinks to break patterns that dominate our lives), and in the rhetoric of creativity it's called creating motifs or recurrent themes.

Cultures have motifs, too. Look at creation myths. Every culture has its distinct and universal pantheon—Sumerian, Aztec, and Roman gods with different names and faces live nearly identical lives (do gods live lives?). Literate societies regularly retell their culture's primitive creation tales. Let's just consider how Western writers have reworked the Book of Genesis. To name only a few, there's Shakespeare's *The Tempest,* Mary Shelley's *Frankenstein,* John Steinbeck's *East of Eden*—not to mention films such as *Metropolis* (Fritz Lang) and *The Ten Commandments* (Cecile B. DeMille). We seem never to tire of telling the story of creation. And yet it's the retelling, the repetition that fascinates. For instance, does this conversation sound familiar?

"Tell me again, Mom."

"But I've told you the story a hundred times."

"Please, just once more."

My mother loves to remind me of when she varied the sacred words of my favorite trickster tale, and I got so angry that I fired her as my personal storyteller. By four years old I already learned that if I wanted a story told right, I'd better do it myself.

The stories we love, the stories that define us, are our sacred wafers. As a poet and an editor, I'm in the ranks of the greatest creation fanatics. The word "poet" is derived from Greek, an early variant of a word that means "maker." And the word "poetry" comes from the word that means, "to make." Authors do make worlds. Poets arguably might have the most developed God complex in the pantheon of demiurges (the Bible and most creation myths are written in poetry). And editors, the redactors of the Bible, who revise, refine, who remain faceless yet an essential force (godlike?), are the next in line after poets with gargantuan creation *cojones*. I say this to let you know, reader, that I am and have always been obsessed with repetition and creation (hence, the early firing of my mother).

When I was a kid—five, six, seven . . . when all of life's possibilities still seemed available to me—more than anything else, I wanted God in my life. I don't mean that I wanted to speak to God and develop a true faith that he was listening. No . . . I wanted to be face-to-face with God: to see God and to hear God directly address me on a first-name basis. The burning bush story was tops. And since God did speak to Moses, logic has it that he could conceivably speak to me. Although many years have passed since I was seven, my desire for God to speak to me is still strong. Really, when one thinks of it, when we write, we are engaged in a dialogue with our forebears . . . those that came and wrote before us . . . our gods and goddesses.

Some of us write directly and consciously with them in mind, some of us write more obliquely, but either way we speak to them, and they to us. *The Tree of Smoke* by Denis Johnson is an homage to Conrad's *Heart of Darkness,* and it draws from the Bible—the title comes from the Book of Joel: "And I will give portents in the heavens and on the earth, blood and fire and palm trees of smoke. The sun shall be turned to darkness, and the moon to blood, before the great and terrible day of the Lord comes." In his novel,

Denis Johnson is in a conversation with every author that ever was, starting with the first author: God.

Writers write in a country, on a continent, of writers. Presently I'm working on a book titled *Mothers, Daughters & Nightbirds: Poems inspired by the Dreams of Emily Dickinson*. My second collection is called *Tales of Murasaki and Other Poems*. When writing *Tales of Murasaki* I used as source material *The Tale of Genji* by Murasaki Shikibu. When writing *The Tale if Genji,* Lady Murasaki was greatly influenced by Confucius (her source material) as well as many poets whose works are recorded in the novel itself. The mutual spirit of creation is alive.

Or is it re-creation that's alive? Or transformation? Let me return again to echolalia. In Ovid's *Metamorphosis*, book three, we first encounter Narcissus and Echo. The story goes that the nymph Echo (who, having lost her ability to choose her words, can only echo others) takes one look at Narcissus and falls in love with him. One day she follows Narcissus to his watering hole, and she sees him call out to his friends.

"Is anyone here?" he asks.

Echo can only reply, "Here."

Narcissus responds, "Come this way," and Echo, with arms open, cries, "This way," and embraces Narcissus.

Narcissus, having no idea that Echo loves him, throws her off, and in the throes of rejection she hides in a cave (where echoes are best suited) and is forever a disembodied voice. Narcissus then sees his visual echo (his reflection) in a pool of water and falls in love with his image. He realizes how impossible his situation is—the loneliness he will always suffer—and pines away staring at his reflection in the pool by the side of the cave. His final heartbreaking farewell is echoed by Echo's voice in the cave. When Narcissus is placed on the funeral pyre, it is said that he was transformed into a Narcissus flower.

You're probably wondering why I offer this tragic story as a celebration of expression. Before and since 8 A.D. (when Ovid wrote the *Metamorphoses)*, people have been running into caves and climbing mountains, shouting at the top of their lungs, surrounded by embracing and magical echoes. They have been singing with abandon in showers and subways. We love our echoes. Echo's heart didn't break because she said the wrong words. In fact, she couldn't have been clearer. What's most heartbreaking about the story is that she utters exactly the right words up to and including her final farewell. Echo's heart breaks because Narcissus was . . . a narcissist. He died because of it, while her voice lives on . . . every writer's dream. And writers, ancient and modern, have been echoing Ovid ever since his telling of this story. Milton retold it in *Paradise Lost,* as did Ben Johnson and Thomas Moore. A continuing stream of contemporary poets, such as Heather McHugh and Fred Chapell, are telling it still.

But what about that little purple flower? That diminutive and fragile life that springs forth (every spring, another echo) . . . from hell knows where. That strange bruised bud is the gift and payoff. I've been given it. I've been in awe of it.

When the first copy of a book that I've written is shipped to me from my publisher with my name printed on the shiny cover, and I crack open the stiff spine to read the first poem, and I think, "How did I write that? No way I'm writing that well today"—when I think I'll never write that well again—I am looking at a field of flowers, bouquets, or gifts from the gods that I've been talking to and, most importantly, who have been talking to me. These flowers printed on creamy paper exist because of them. They are my burning bush. As a writer, I get to speak to the gods—face-to-face—and sometimes when I look into a quiet pool of water, they offer me a flower. Unlike Narcissus I could never fall in love with myself because I know to thank the gods for the small miracles that have been bestowed upon me in the shape of a flower, in the sound of an echo.

We Make It All Up Anyway . . . Might as Well Make It Up Good!

Laura Duksta

These sound like words from a good ol' country song, but they are also words that I live by. It wasn't too long ago that I realized the power of our word and how our words along with our thoughts and beliefs actually create our world. I realized that this power had always been at work in my life but it was happening unconsciously and with no direction. Over the past several years I have become conscious of the power of my word and have been using this awareness to consciously co-create the life of my dreams. I have also been blessed with the opportunity to share with others, including young people and educators, how to achieve their dreams and transform their lives by harnessing the power of their word. You are writing the story of your life. Are you writing one that empowers you or a dark comedy with a tragic ending?

When I was 11 years old, I developed a condition that caused all of my waist-length, wavy brown hair to fall out. It was a terrible experience. It started out as a small, nickel-sized patch at the back right side of my scalp, small enough that it was hidden and easy enough to deny. My cousin noticed it one day while braiding my hair, and I blew it off as nothing important, refusing to acknowledge its existence. Within a few months, though, I was an 11-year-old with a really bad "comb over," desperately trying to cover up the bald patches that were shining through my hair that was now falling out in clumps.

My mother brought me to several doctors before getting a diagnosis of *Alopecia areata universalis*, a very pretty name for "total hair loss." The doctor at Boston Children's Hospital said, "There isn't much you can do. Get her a wig and no one needs to know." My mother didn't think this was great advice, but I was happy to go along with it as I began to close down emotionally. Quickly I went from being an outgoing child to someone who barely wanted to speak or to be seen. People acted like there was something wrong with me, and that is how I felt.

I decided, "I am never going to have friends, nobody will ever like me, and I will never be able to do all the things I dream of doing." What I didn't realize is that the more I thought like this, the more these ideas became my reality. People found it difficult to get close to me; it was hard to get me to open up, and I began shying away from the singing, performing, and dancing that I loved so much.

Slowly, over the years, I realized that I was learning lessons about love, compassion, and understanding for humanity through my experience of being bald, lessons that I probably wouldn't trade for my hair. Still, I never let anyone see me without a wig on, and I didn't even look at myself in a mirror bald for ten full years! I felt ashamed of myself and therefore people around me felt ashamed and/or sorry for me. For 19 long years I wore wigs, and it wasn't until an experience of divine inspiration that I got the courage to shed my wigs and set myself free. It was just weeks before my 30th birthday when, out of nowhere, I decided that I was no longer going to wear wigs. I told my friends to throw me a big party in NYC at Life nightclub, and we would have what has now become known as my "Coming Out Party" as "The Bald Chick." No longer hiding created a certain sense of freedom for me, but along with that there was still a feeling of being somewhat uncomfortable in my own skin.

It wasn't until I did an exercise at a seminar I was attending that I began to see how I was creating my world through my thoughts, beliefs, and words. The instructors asked us to look at what had been the most difficult situation in our lives. That was easy for me: losing my hair, although I had also had to deal with my best friend dying in a car accident and growing up in what would be called a pretty abusive/dysfunctional family. But they said to pick one, so I went with my hair. They asked us to separate out what the facts were from the story we made up about it. You know when the police say, "Just the facts ma'am," they are trying to have you let go of the story, meaning, and emotion that you are adding to what actually is. The only facts in my story were that I lost all of my hair at the age of 11. Everything else that I ever said about it or that others said about it and agreed with was meaning that we added to the actual facts.

Next, the instructors encouraged me to make up a completely different meaning for why I lost my hair and what was going to happen because I lost my hair. That's when the exercise got fun. They asked me to make up the most obscure and funny reason I had lost my hair. I explained that I was from another planet. I was an alien who had come to enlighten the rest of the world. But it would be important for me first to appear to be just like human beings, and now that it was almost time for me to do my work and return home, it was time for me to allow my natural looks to shine through.

The fact was that I had lost my hair; all the stories I made up were just stories, the ones I believed or the ones I newly created. Now the alien story wasn't true either, but I began to realize that I could make a story that would keep me down and depressed or I could create a story that empowers and inspires me.

Soon, I began to change my world by saying things like, "I lost my hair when I was 11, but besides having no hair, I am perfectly healthy. Losing my hair has been the greatest gift in that it has taught me lessons of love, understanding, and compassion for humanity." Shortly after shifting my inner story I self-published a book called *I Love You More*. To my new empowering story, I added, "I get to go into schools and share with young people about self-esteem and love and the powerful, though not always easy, lesson to Just Be Yourself. As an author, being bald makes me memorable and marketable." Again, none of this *is* the truth. I still have the same bald head, but now the story I have made up is one that serves me rather than stops me.

What stories are you holding onto that no longer serve you? The stories we make up or buy into, especially when we are young, are often ones that are passed onto us by our families, our cultures, our class, our race, and other groups we're in. I know this is not always easy to do, but I believe with every part of my being that it is fully possible. You can change your words, thoughts, and beliefs and create a whole new experience for yourself and your life. Now, it can happen instantly, but often there will be some work to do. When you have lost a job, gone through a divorce, have had to deal with the loss of a loved one, or been in an "abusive" relationship, there are a lot of people who will agree with you that these are tragic, abusive, unfair, difficult circumstances. But when you can separate out what actually happened from the meaning you have given it and consciously create a new meaning—one that empowers you—you will find yourself no longer stuck by the situation that once stopped you. Often this will take sharing with others that you have created a new and improved version of your story. Consider that your biography was sent off to an editor and after a quick revision you came back a superhero!

Are you still unwilling to let go of some of your old stuff? There are two other super powers of creativity in the universe: love and gratitude! They work in a similar way to changing your story, but reach a little deeper for those of you who might be holding on tight. I believe that our biggest challenges become our biggest blessings when we allow them to. I gradually began to see this for myself when going through my teens and 20s. I realized the life lessons that I was learning I would not trade for my hair. It was after working with my mentor and colleague John DeMartini, Ph.D., that I experienced this on an even greater level and can now say with utmost certainty that there is not a person, situation, or event that we cannot put into our heart and become grateful for. When we are grateful for something, someone, or some experience that we have been festering resentment, anger, unforgiveness, or hatred towards, we immediately dissolve the charge and become free. We bring light to the situation and rise above what has kept us down.

Gratitude and love exist at a centered space of being. They exist in the now moment. When you are letting emotions from the past run your life, you keep yourself from the grace of the now moment. In truth, we can be controlled as easily from positive charges as negative charges, although one feels like depression and the other elation, which can at least temporarily feel great. Once we bring ourselves back to a balanced state, we are now aligned with our true self and can express the highest vision for our life.

Here is an exercise to clear out the negative (or positive) charge around a person, situation, or event. This can be a little more work, and at times uncomfortable, but if you do it you will experience a sense of freedom, lightness, and grace. You will want to write down at least 10–20 attributes that "push your buttons" about the person, situation, or event. For example, "abusive, manipulative, draining, and controlling." Now, here comes the kicker. You have to bring back to memory times when people have *perceived* you in this same way. It might help to jot down their initials. The next step is to write down how this person being this way has served you, and then how your being this way has served others.

Impossible, you might think. But if you get to work and dig, at the end of the exercise you will experience the magical power of gratitude and love. You will be rewriting your story when you realize that the people, events, and experiences that caused you the most grief in your life have often also been the catalyst to your greatest growth and awareness.

Through rewriting my own story I have become realigned with my higher self and my life purpose, which is to travel the world, meet my brothers and sisters, and spread the message of love. It is amazing how many ways have been made available for me to fulfill this mission. I have my *New York Times* bestselling book, *I Love You More,* which has sold close to 250,000 copies. The book and its message of love are in the hearts, homes, and classrooms of loved ones all over the world.

In addition, my music with a message is being played throughout cyberspace, and it is currently being remixed by one of the worlds top DJ's. I have the opportunity to speak with students, parents, educators, and organizations about the capacity of human potential and universal laws and principles that they can consciously align with and use to express their highest vision for themselves. I am co-founder of a global web community called Co-creating Our Reality, representing people from over 125 countries who are taking responsibility for writing their own story and co-creating their lives through the power of their word, thoughts and beliefs. If you are a fan of *The Secret*, *A New Earth*, Abraham, Wayne Dyer, and so on, you will love Co-creating Our Reality and The 100-Day Reality Challenge. I welcome you to check out this community and begin to align with and live your life's true purpose.

Remember we make it all up anyway, so we might as well make it up good! As soon as I shifted from a story that stopped me for many years to one that empowers me I have found endless ways to generate the conversation of love around the world . . . through books, music, speaking, TV, film, and the web! Create a game worth playing and go out and have some fun. And if you, your organization, or your school could use a dose of love and inspiration, well, call me. That's my job. I would be happy to help you along on your journey.

Have a bright and blessed lifetime. Keep shining!

How "Positive" Is Positive Thinking?

Robert and Michelle Colt

Positive thinking is the new mantra leading a great resurgence of interest in the field of personal development. While the power of positive thinking is certainly not a new theme, a vast, collective marketing machine has brought the positive thinking movement greater attention than ever before. Movies like *The Secret* and *What the Bleep Do We Know?!* have spun the power of positive thinking to such a degree that many major corporations are now using it as the central concept in their advertising campaigns. But does positive thinking really work? Is it neurologically possible? Is it healthy? And if it isn't, how positive is positive thinking?

Let's look at quantum physics. We know through the discoveries made by quantum scientists that what we perceive to be a solid world isn't really solid at all. It's mostly space. The nature of our senses combined with the rate of speed of atoms spinning creates the illusion of a solid world. Think of an electric fan for a moment. When it's turned off you can easily see the space between the blades. Turn it on and it clearly appears to be solid. The spinning of atoms creates a similar illusion.

If you were to put on a quantum lens as you're reading this essay, the words, as well as your immediate environment, would instantly disappear.

What you'd see instead would be mostly space with an occasional particle floating by. How would you know where to move, sit, or direct your attention? It would be utter chaos.

This is where the brain and nervous system come into play. The human nervous system, of which the brain is the primary organ, has two primary functions. First, it is in charge of our perceptions of order and chaos. Second, it handles matters related to survival and security. Every second there are 400 billion bytes of information coming in through our neurology, mainly as space or nothingness. To deal with this chaos and survive, the brain/nervous system omits, omits, omits, omits most of the nothingness and abstracts out 0.000054 percent of what's really there. We then call this our reality.

For a moment, look at all the life forms around you, including you, as energy expressing itself in unique patterns of subatomic particles. While the atoms, electrons, and molecules that make "you" up are the same building blocks used in all forms, it is the particular combination of subatomic particles that create an endless stream of unique life forms. Take your body for a moment. The combinations of subatomic particles that make up your heart are quite different than those of your liver. The atoms of each are spinning at different rates and vibrations, which result in specific and unique functioning.

What does any of this have to do with positive thinking? Thoughts also represent a unique vibration of subatomic patterning, called *binary* or *dualistic patterning*. This simply means that every thought arises with its seeming opposite as a unit. Good simultaneously arises with bad, right simultaneously arises with wrong, black with white, and so on. For our purposes, it would be more accurate to read them as goodbad, rightwrong, and blackwhite, because they are single units in the thought system.

On a practical level these pairs of seeming opposites allow for distinctions to be made. How would you know what front is without back, light without dark, love without hate? As you can see, they serve an important purpose. Without the nervous system's omission/abstraction process and these binary units of thought, everything would just be one big indistinguishable mass of nothingness. Imagine trying to meet friends at your favorite restaurant. Good luck.

Clearly there's a great misunderstanding going on amid people in the power of positive thinking movement, because they have dedicated themselves to only half of the pattern. If love arises with hate and I'm told only to think of love, does hate eventually dissolve and disappear? And if it doesn't disappear, where does it go? Let's look at the ramifications of this lack of understanding.

The illusion that hate disappears if we don't focus on it is not too dissimilar from the illusion that the nothingness disappears in the omission and abstraction process discussed earlier. What actually happens is that "hate" becomes marginalized. This marginalization varies to different degrees, depending on the power and commitment we employ in forcing this unnatural illusion.

In the binary unit of lovehate, positive thinking attempts to do the impossible: to separate the two halves of the pair and have one kill off the other. In this case, love attempts to destroy hate. But in an act of non-violence (love), great violence is taking place. This can be experienced in the physical body as stress, tension, or some form of somatic discomfort. On a psychological level, it is often experienced as a sense of failure, shame, and eventually resignation.

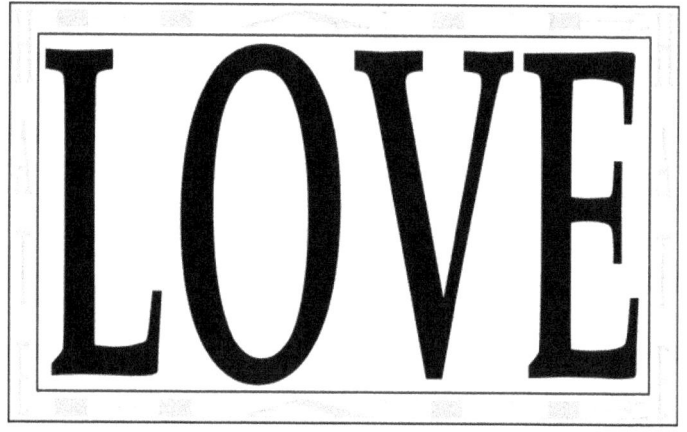

It's unfortunate that the person getting involved in positive thinking is unaware of the setup to fail from the onset, because positive thinking is an unnatural process. Positive thinking, by the very nature of the subatomic patterning of thoughts, is an ideal that cannot possibly be lived up to. This would be like expecting your liver to perform the function of your heart.

To add further light to the "dark side" of positive thinking, let's turn the clock back to 2,000 B.C. and the teachings of the founder of Madhyamika

Buddhism, a man named Nagarjuna. What we've been describing as units of binary thoughts, Nagarjuna called "dependent origination." He went on to say that everything in the manifest world arises dependently and therefore has no independent nature. Life is a living unit or what quantum physicists call a *unified field*. It's important to note that what Nagarjuna discovered in 2,000 B.C quantum physicists discovered close to 4,000 years later.

Earlier we said that the brain/nervous system has two primary paradigmatic functions: 1. Order/chaos, 2. Security/survival. Let's now look at its second function. As we grow and develop, the survival/security mechanism of the nervous system expresses itself through the actions fight, flight, freeze, and pray. The father of quantum psychology, Stephen Wolinsky, added "pray" to the list created by behaviorists, and he reminds us, "There are no atheists in foxholes."

Basically, everything our brain/nervous system does it does for survival. So let's go back to the original question posed at the top of this essay. When we are sold on the non-viable paradigm of "positive thinking," are there any consequences in regards to the natural functioning of the brain/nervous system's hard-wiring to survive at all costs? If positive thinking is an unlivable ideal, how does that affect our connection with the innate intelligence of the brain/nervous system? Does it even matter?

The fact that the brain/nervous system is hard-wired for security/survival is not going to change. That's a subatomic and physiological constant. Here's where the problem lies. By doing something completely unnatural ("positive" thinking) we are cut off from the very fabric of intelligence itself.

Pause for a moment and ponder the following questions. Are you beating your heart or is it just beating? Do you grow your hair and fingernails or do they grow on their own? After you eat a meal, do you have to give orders to your gastrointestinal tract to digest your food?

Notice how the tides come in and go out, how the seasons change, and how the planets revolve around the Sun. Ponder the vastness of multiple galaxies, the subatomic world, and the very fact that you are alive. Think of the intelligence involved in this awesome livingness.

Do you think this intelligence "screwed up" in regards to patterning thoughts as binary units? The problem is not in the nature of thought itself. The problem is going against this nature and not allowing thoughts to flow freely in their natural units. The mistake is buying into the "lie" that you can actually choose one side (there are no sides) of the unit over the other. That the good in goodbad can actually wipe out the bad.

Any attempt to go against what is the natural functioning only serves to further remove us from it.

Here's the paradox and the solution. When we begin to understand and become more comfortable with the binary nature of thoughts, a fascinating occurrence happens. The thoughts lose the discordant charge they once had as a result of the former false polarization, and what emerges is an underlying essence often described as peace, joy, spaciousness, and connection.

In place of positive thinking comes a capacity for clear reasoning, genuine intimacy, a body at-ease, rather than in dis-ease, and deep relaxation of the brain/nervous system, which no longer perceives *itself* (through falsely divided thoughts) as a threat.

No matter what you do, the world will continue to spin, as the world spins: with its goodbads, updowns, lightdarks, lovehates. As you see through the illusion of "positive thinking," it will become significantly apparent as the Third Ch'an Patriarch Seng'stan said, "The Great Way knows no difficulties except for those who have preferences."

Soul Currency—
Invest Your Inner Wealth

Ernest D. Chu

How creative do you have to be to thrive with the prospect of $5-plus per gallon gas and rising prices for just about everything?

You may already be feeling a twinge of fear as you look at what's barely left of your paycheck at the end of the month, or when you spend nearly $70 or more to fill up the car at the gas station. The rising prices of virtually anything that is affected by petroleum products (which is nearly everything) is like an unexpected tax of an additional 15 percent more of spendable income. You can't immediately depend on cost of living adjustments to bring things back to normal as salary adjustments typically trail rising prices by three years or more.

These are not just challenging times. We are likely to be entering into a prolonged period of economic and social change during which we will be paying for excesses such as real estate and world consumption of key commodities that we have long taken for granted. So what does this mean to you and investing your inner wealth? Just about everything! Never before has creativity been more important, as the next few years will be a continuation of one of the biggest periods of redistribution of wealth in history. Will you benefit from these changing times or will you allow yourself to be a victim of circumstances?

Instead of focusing on circumstances, such as the major changes in the drastic increases in energy, commodities, and transportation, or the drastically lower re-pricing of the housing, building, and stock market sectors, it is time to focus on the enormous and generally underutilized asset within: your inner assets, a part of your soul currency.

Your Spiritual Assets

In my book *Soul Currency: Investing Your Inner Wealth for Fulfillment and Abundance,* I've categorized inner spiritual assets into four categories: Intuition and Guidance, Creativity, Higher Personality Traits, and Cultivated Skills and Knowledge. As a former securities analyst and corporate chief financial officer, I know that even though these assets might seem intangible, they are critical to your ability to set and achieve goals, to dream and envision, and to be in the flow of an intelligent and alive universe that responds to our empowering, positive thoughts and to our negative, limiting beliefs.

In challenging times, it is especially important that you look within, see, and remove limiting beliefs, hold on to empowering thoughts, which become actions, and through intention and focus, activate those assets to ride the wave of change rather than to be buried by it. Let's look at our spiritual assets category by category.

1. *Intuition and Guidance.* Many of the world's most successful people, including government leaders and chief executives, reply upon intuition and guidance to help them make important decisions, assess colleagues and adversaries, and navigate their way through business opportunities and problems. Intuition is a knowing voice that originates from deep inside of us. People experience intuition in different ways, but there is nearly always a sense of "rightness" about intuition, a feeling of having penetrated beyond the obvious surface layer of the world. One example of intuition in action might be a securities analyst who had the feeling that a company he was covering was having trouble with its orders. Yet management seemed perpetually optimistic. In a dream, he saw the company's stock down nearly 90 percent. The next day he continued to dig around for reasons why that might happen until he talked to one of the company's customers, who told him that the company was unable to deliver its new product. Another example of the intuitive urge could simply be feeling a desire to take a more scenic route home than usual, thus avoiding a significant unreported accident that tied up the highway for hours.

2. *Creativity.* In its many forms, creativity is one of your greatest inner assets. When you feel inspired by ideas, you are swept up in Spirit's creative flow, your imagination is stimulated, and you express yourself consciously and unconsciously as Spirit moves through you. Creativity is not limited to the obvious, such as the ability to write, to compose and play music, and to dance, or to being able to access artistic inspiration and endeavors. One of my dorm mates at Amherst was Dr. Peter B. Wylie, now one of the country's leading industrial psychologists. Even though he was a psychology major, one of his real loves was statistics. And although he was trained in industrial psychology, he always was fascinated by education. Nearly a decade ago, he noticed that universities and other educational institutions that are perpetually dependent on donations had huge databases, which they never did much with. With novel ways of data-mining these enormous troves of information, Peter innovated the use of new techniques for dramatically increasing fundraising and development of donors. Another example of someone who puts the asset of creativity into action is the former credit market and insurance specialist Lee Van Slyke, a man who saw an opportunity to develop a system for reducing volatility in commodities and other related trading through a novel method of reinsuring risk.

3. *Higher Personality Traits.* Sometimes called character traits, the higher personality traits stem from our personal values. They are fundamental in achieving success in any endeavor. In his book *Learned Optimism*, Dr. Martin Seligman, one of the fathers of the field of positive psychology, offers the theory of flexible optimism that allows us to discern the positive aspects of all situations. Quantum physics has begun to demonstrate that our higher personality traits, such as persistence, courage, integrity, optimism, and so forth, are reflected in our reality.

4. Cultivated Skills and Knowledge. You can add cultivated skills and knowledge, such as those gained from a high school or college education or professional or technical training, to your list of spiritual assets. Also add physical conditioning and wisdom. How these skills eventually factor into your career and success may surprise you. Steve Jobs, the founder of Apple Computer, reportedly said that he applied skills he learned in a calligraphy course at Reed College in Portland, Oregon, to his design for the original Apple computer. Dr. Dan Carlson, inventor of the Sonic Bloom technology that creates significantly larger crop harvests, discovered how to use new techniques through his studies and subsequent work at the University of Minnesota's Experimental College where he designed his own curriculum in horticulture and agriculture.

If there is so much wealth hidden in our spiritual assets, what do we have to do to activate it? As a Wall Street investment-banking executive for many years, I've known that unless assets are invested, they become dormant and even lose value. When assets, such as funds, are invested, they unleash the power of capital to create companies, build new industries, like biotechnology and the Internet industry, and create billions in stock market value. But as a business and life coach and a spiritual teacher, I have realized that we can do the same thing on a much larger scale with our own inner assets. When we activate our spiritual assets, we create a wealth that lies within us: spiritual or inner capital, which is really the source of all capital (including financial, social, intellectual, and human capital).

Learning how to awaken and invest this tremendous inner wealth will enable you reach your goals, increase your income, and find deep personal fulfillment.

Creating Spiritual Capital

As an investment advisor, I used to focus initially on what type of return I could create for my clients, and then I'd assess the risks and rewards. I added my personal intuition and insight to the mix. Most of the time if my team had "done our homework," that is, if we'd focused on the investment and our intention was clear, we'd be successful. The discipline was to get out when the original reasons for getting into the investment changed—regardless of how big the gain and whether or not there was loss.

Investing spiritual capital is similar to cash investments since the symbols of value, such as financial currency, stocks, and bonds, all have been agreements on value that have emerged from our spiritual capital. To create spiritual capital you must be clear about your intentions, as our individual connections connect us to a deeper field of intentionality (an aspect of the universal source energy). A butterfly has the intention to alight on a flower and feed on its nectar. Intentionality is built into the butterfly species, whose members all travel up to 3,000 miles to spend the winter in a warmer climate.

Focus is a spiritual asset, which we often call by other names: determination, attention, commitment, concentration, and single-mindedness. It's what makes the goal-setting process work in life and in business, and it is responsible for any occasion in which you may recall asserting, "When I really make up my mind that I want something, I get it!" But focus is also the process of noticing present time, of reorganizing potential into thought, of taking action, and finally of manifesting into outcome.

The Hidden Power in Soul Currency

The key ingredient to spiritual capital that distinguishes it from financial capital is love, which is the source energy of our universe. Love is not a feeling that comes from within us; rather it is the creative power of an infinite source energy that moves through and activates everything. It is a creative force that has an intelligence of its own, which intensifies focus and enriches our intentions. Life imitates Spirit, and the flow of financial currency imitates the flow of love, the soul's currency. Being in the "flow" is therefore to be in the flow of soul currency.

Tapping into this extraordinary power is what enables entrepreneur extraordinaire Donald Trump, a man who lives for the challenge of a great deal, to find a way to get an especially intractable and lucrative deal done, or for Susan Lindstrom, founder of Paper Source, to innovate a chain of stores based on her love for artistic presentation. She used love to find a way to sell fine handmade papers with great unusual colors and designs. While going through her mother's personal effects after she had passed away, Lindstrom began to appreciate what a cherished gift handwritten letters could be. Her company has partnered in supporting The Campaign for Love and Forgiveness to support the organization's letter writing initiative.

The energy of love is also a powerful creative impetus for Sandra Muvdi, whose only child, seven-year-old Jessica June Eilers, died of acute leukemia in 2003. Her grief and love for her daughter led her to found the Jessica June Children's Cancer Foundation, whose mission is "giving hope and comfort to underprivileged children with cancer."

Creating with Soul Currency

Your spiritual capital is creative, alive, and more powerful than money because it is infused with the source energy of love. For those who like formulas, the equation for spiritual capital is: $SC = (F + I + SA)^L$ or: spiritual capital equals focus plus intentionality plus spiritual assets, all multiplied exponentially by love.

As you begin creating your spiritual capital, focus on contributing your spiritual assets rather than on being attached to the form in which your returns come back. When you invest spiritual capital, you create the conditions. The outcomes are often unexpectedly better than you imagined. Returning to the question I asked in the beginning, "How creative do you have to be to thrive in changing and challenging times?" here are four suggestions for creating your life in a new socioeconomic world.

Share What Is Uniquely Yours with the World

Each of us has many choices of how we create income. Most of us spend the majority of our waking time in work-related activities. If you look at work as simply an activity that generates a paycheck, then ultimately you will have to find meaning in other parts of your life. Do what you enjoy and remember that even if you enjoy helping people, you don't necessarily have to work in a not-for-profit company. Recognize that it is what you bring to your work rather than solely the work itself that is a major part of that experience. When you begin to value yourself and what you have to offer, you will ultimately share with the world what is uniquely yours.

When British author J.K. Rowling created the Harry Potter series of books, she wrote her first book having to rely on what little savings she had and some public assistance. But her most valuable investment was her great imagination, her ability to paint pictures with words and to envision a fantasy world of Muggles, Wizards, and dragons. Many of Rowling's friends and neighbors certainly had some doubts as to whether she ever would make any money as a writer. Yet, within ten years, Rowling's unique Harry Potter brand, encompassing several books, movies, and ancillary products, was worth several billion dollars, a return on investment that dwarfed even the returns on investment by the early shareholders of Microsoft.

Come from Your Strengths

When I was growing up, I was ashamed of the fact that I looked different and was shorter than my classmates. What I would have given to be six-foot tall with blonde hair and blue eyes rather than being five-foot-six and Chinese-American. But when I went to Wall Street, one of the hottest fund managers at the time was Gerald Tsai, a Chinese-American who had been born in Shanghai. I discovered not only that it was okay to be Chinese, but also that there were quite a few advantages to it. I could walk into a crowded room and, while I might have some difficulty remembering everyone, almost everyone would remember me. I had inherited a solid work ethic and part of my gifts was my ability to take in what might be an overwhelming amount of information and not only to sort it out, but also to glean insights from it.

Steve Jobs, the founder of Apple Computer and Pixar Studios, had the gift of being able to blend creativity with precision and insight with imagination. Apple, which has competed against giants like Microsoft, HP, Toshiba, Sony, and IBM, not only gained a substantial market share, it has built generations of loyal Apple users. The collective investment of the founding group in both Apple and Pixar created the inspiration for the products, the impetus for their funding, and enabled these companies to become the innovation leaders in computers and computer-generated entertainment.

Invest Your Soul Currency

When you use your inner assets, direct them with intention and focus. You only need to add the source energy of love to harness spiritual capital. The feeling of love, which is the soul's real currency, is more than a feeling of well-being. It is creative, connective, and transformative. When you invest your spiritual capital, the return on investment is not simply monetary, it also opens up other possibilities.

My good friend and mentor, the late Jay Wells, always looked for opportunities to help people. He made friends easily because he was interested in others, a quality that helped him become a successful businessman. One day, Wells found himself hospitalized for a routine procedure. When he was recovering, he started talking to some of the nurses and other patients, asked why there weren't any TVs in the hospital. He was told that there was one in the doctor's lounge and that TVs were a luxury that the hospital couldn't afford. He began by offering to donate a few televisions to the hospital, and eventually this led to formation of Wells National Services, a public company that became the leader in installing and renting bedside televisions to hospital patients.

Joel Roberts, one of this country's top media coaches, is another example of investing soul currency. For more than 15 years, Roberts was the feisty, sarcastic, and often deliberately controversial drive-time radio host of one of the top-rated stations in the country: Los Angeles-based KABC. A music aficionado, Roberts found himself at a concert standing near one of the huge speakers when it accidentally blew out, causing him to lose most of his hearing in one ear and more than 60 percent in the other. From the top of his profession, he suddenly was unemployed. Or so he thought. Today Roberts is one of world's top message and media coaches. He helps authors, executives, salesmen, lawyers, and publicists apply some of the same skills he used on the air, such as having a hard-hitting message, holding listener interest, and learning how to use news headlines to build a hook.

Living from Flow

Soul currency investing is so much more powerful than the limiting aspects of simply investing the symbols that represent money. Soul currency enables us to live from possibility rather than investing from fear and risk. From an open heart, we are able to share and to put ourselves in the flow of not only material prosperity, but also the deep fulfillment and inevitable right action that love always produces. The message we receive is one of greater connection, not only to others around and the collective good, but to a deeper inner connection to Spirit that brings us fulfillment and a sense of greater purpose.

The Wizard Within

C. Russell Brumfield

You are a creative being in a perpetual process of creativity. It doesn't matter how you earn your living or spend your days. You could be an accountant, a project manager, a restaurant server, or a homemaker. There is no time when you are not molding and sculpting the material conditions and experiences in your life. But you may doubt it, like so many people do. You may even respond negatively when asked if you can sing, write, paint, or dance. It's possible that you once aspired to work in a creative field but dropped the intention after succumbing to constant doubts about your talent.

In a study of a kindergarten class, the children were asked to raise their hands for a positive response to certain questions. When the researcher asked the class, "Who can sing?" all the students raised their hands. When asked who could dance, paint, or tell stories, again there was a resounding affirmative response. A decade later the researchers returned to the same students to pose the same questions. The differences were startling. When each question was posed, only a few brave souls raised their hands in response. This demonstration speaks volumes about human nature and how society inhibits it.

Essentially, we start out our lives as creative little humans with the absolute belief that we can do anything. Then society slowly strips away our confidence in our creative abilities until we finally believe we are devoid of talent and ingenuity. Luckily, many of us are taught that everyone has at least one "God-given" talent, so we don't lose all hope during our formative years. We are merely inhibited by indoctrination.

I immediately identified with the aforementioned study when I discovered it, for I was one of the societal statistics that the researchers noted. I spent my formative years feeling that I lacked true creativity, and thus I initially chose to study medicine, a field where I could employ the one "divinely gifted" talent: intelligence. I entered the Air Force as a flying medic in order to afford the schooling to obtain a medical degree. But after four years of spending my days in my craft and my nights in my studies, I changed my direction to the utter dismay of my family and friends. Although I found emergency medicine interesting, I had lost all passion for it. And at this very critical stage of my life, I knew that whatever I chose as a field of endeavor would need to be something that I could be passionate about. I just didn't have any idea what it was.

I skipped finishing my pre-med degree and, to my mother's absolute horror, became a fast-food restaurant manager after my discharge from the military. It didn't matter to her that paramedics made $13,000 a year (in 1982) and that I had landed a

$20,000 per year salary. I jumped into the job with all of the passion I could muster and quickly moved up the corporate ladder. Eighteen months later, I lost my passion for a second time. But at least I realized why this had happened to me twice in six years.

I came to the solid conclusion that I couldn't follow the traditional path of working in a corporate structure where I had to work for people who really weren't all that smart or where others had personal agendas that were far more important to them than the ultimate success of the company. I had grown tired of vying for promotion by coming up with innovative measures to improve costs and efficiency, only to be rejected by a superior whose sole explanation for the rejection was, "That's not the way we do it here."

The reason I lost my passion for the military, for medicine, and for the food and beverage business was the same: There was little room for thinking outside of the box. Period. Thus, I decided to switch gears once again. At the ripe old age of 24, I left the "box" for parts unknown in search of my passion. I spent six long months (a long time to a 24-year-old) contemplating my entrepreneurial capabilities. The fact that I was broke and sharing an apartment with two other people would not help in my pursuit. But I was determined to strike out on my own. I looked into the lawn mowing business and assisted care, and even into opening a counseling business, three fields where I had experience.

Finally, my parents suggested that I do some catering out of their 30-seat deli. It was closed after 5 P.M., so I would be able to have the kitchen for myself.

The idea only came about because I had used the kitchen to make some party platters for a friend's wedding during my sabbatical and my mother had noticed that I enjoyed doing it. I soon found myself picking my first entrepreneurial venture as a caterer. I jumped into it with the fiery passion of a preacher on the pulpit south of the Mason-Dixon Line.

I did what came naturally. I headed to the library to study the catering business. I found a single book on the subject, *Cater from Your Kitchen* by Marjorie Blanchard (Bobbs-Merrill, 1981). I read the book in one evening, and I was devastated at what the author said was the key ingredient to becoming a successful caterer. As I recall, the fateful line went something like this: "Highly successful caterers are known for their creativity." This one statement stopped me dead in my tracks. My immediate thought was, "What am I going to do . . . because I am certainly not creative?" I remember that day back in 1984, and the ensuing days spent carrying around the feeling that I had once again chosen the wrong career. Then, serendipitously, I was fortunate to pick up another book that got my mind off of my dilemma: *The Magic of Thinking Big* by David Schwartz (Fireside, 1987). This little tome literally changed my life and my thinking.

Reading well-explained concepts like believe and succeed, you are what you think you are, think positive, and turn defeat into victory, I shifted the gears in my thinking and thereby immediately changed my life. I vowed never again to make the statement that I was not a creative person, and instead to start to affirm to myself that I was the most creative person in the catering business. I kept this vow and I've never looked back.

Five years later, I counted that I had planned and executed over a thousand weddings. Nineteen years later, I had executed over 15,000 theme parties and had designed themed restaurants and theme park environments all over the world. What was my moniker in the industry? For 20 years I was known as "The Wizard," and I ran a company called Wizard Studios. It takes some pretty big *cojones* to put down "Wizard" as your title on a business card, but I had regained my mojo: the confidence I had lost in my childhood. Once I had learned that creativity is an innate element in all of us and that all I needed to do was to tap into my personal supply from the Divine Artist, I was able to spend the subsequent 20 years upping my creativity quotient. Let me share what I have learned.

First, let's take a look at how personal experience compares to the universe's natural processes. Every object in nature either is growing and emerging or is contracting and dying. No matter what you observe in nature, from the flora and the fauna on down to the tiniest cell, this is evident. For now, even the universe is expanding, although scientists predict that it eventually and naturally will contract. As we observe nature, every element within it encounters this element of expansion and contraction.

There is a point in the human lifespan beyond which we cease to grow physically. Then our bodies begin to age and recede, initiating the process that will culminate in our death. Like the human condition, this cyclical process is true in every corner of nature.

Cities, civilizations, economies, trends, and religions go through this same process. In fact, every condition and experience will go through this cycle. In essence, you are either emerging (growing) in your experience or descending (dying).

Look around you and notice the people in your life. They will show signs of which specific slope they are traveling. We can see a passionate fire burning in some people (young or old) whom we admire for their effervescence, energy, and the ardent stances that they take in their every endeavor. We all have people in our lives that emulate these qualities. We consider them special. We can also see those who seem to have lost their flicker. These folks are in a rut. They face constant strife and struggle and seem devoid of passion. But the question is not really about them; it's about us.

Do you have the same burning desires of emergence that you once had? Do you hold a thirst for knowledge? Are you flowing with love for others? Are you on fire to explore new realms, new cultures, and new ideas? Or do you feel that your time has passed or that you missed the boat? Have you come to the conclusion that desires and yearnings are merely musings of the young and foolish?

Here's one more, simple question: Are you growing or are you dying? If your answer is positive, then congratulations—you are probably successful in your creative pursuits. If you find yourself deliberating the question, then we have uncovered a key element that is a primary block to your creative process. Passion, curiosity, and an unquenched thirst for the next adventure are energetic qualities necessary for harnessing your true creative potential. It is important to evaluate your condition in order to tap into the creative formulas of the universe and to develop and hone your inner artist, or what I call the Wizard within.

As stated above, we are all creative beings living in a 24/7 cycle of a creative universe. The universe is made up of only two real elements—thought and energy that are molded into matter. Quantum physicists have shown that matter is influenced by thought, which is well on the way to being proved to be the foundation of matter. In essence, every physical object is formed by thought. The universe is comprised of the seen (infinite atoms formed into physical properties) and the unseen (ever-creative influencing thought). This is pretty simple, really, once you apply the universal laws.

After years of studying the elements that go into the phenomenon of manifestation from unseen to seen, I have broken them down into five requisite conditions:

- **Concept.** No invention was ever brought about without it first being held in mind as a concept. Think of the wheel or any form of shelter or clothing, the light bulb, the airplane, or even the chair where you are sitting. Before these items ever came into existence, they were first conceived in the mind. This first law of creativity is the easiest to grasp, for we all conceive thousands of ideas in our lifetimes. Most of these concepts die quickly, fading into the ethers, for they fail to progress to the next stage of creativity, which is *definition*, or what I call *blueprinting*.

- **Definition (or Blueprint).** All man-made creations are well defined and blueprinted long before they become a reality (the same can be said for human-made conditions, as we'll soon see). In order for a car to become a car, a house to become a house, and a cup to become a cup, these things must first be defined visually in the mind or on paper. All of the human creations that have been invented since we arrived on planet Earth were first conceived and defined, with no exceptions. Nonetheless, there have been trillions of blueprinted plans and defined visualizations that have never made it to fruition in history due to the absence of the next law: *inspiration*.
- **Inspiration.** Inspiration literally means, *"breathing life into."* In actuality, inspiration brings an idea or a concept into existence. However, an inspired idea will rapidly die without a maintained inspiration that carries it through to its physical manifestation. Inspiration can be identified as passion, emotion, or feeling—which brings us back to why we may feel stuck when we have lost our passion. Again, no invention has been brought to existence without the inspirational efforts of the individual. Thomas Edison performed 10,000 experiments before finally creating the incandescent light bulb. Interestingly, he was the lone individual who was sufficiently inspired to develop a concept that had been originated by others more than 50 years before. What inspired Edison to carry out a mind-boggling 10,000 experiments? His passion, driven

by the next law of creative manifestation, was *desire*.
- **Desire.** Desire and inspiration may seem to be similar to the naked eye, but they are actually two progressive elements. Desire is a product of inspiration. But one can be inspired about a concept and yet lack the desire to see it through. We might also call desire *motivation*. The world is full of mediocre artists, writers, and performers who never finish their projects due to the inherent absence of powerful desire. Again, we could recite infinite examples of ideas that were conceived, defined, blueprinted, and inspired—initially—only to be doomed to the bottom drawer by the absence of motivation and desire. Yet even if we employ the first four laws, we are still missing the most important key to manifesting any item or condition: *expectation*.
- **Expectation.** Lack of expectation is the culprit in most failed creative attempts. We all know people who constantly have some pretty great ideas, and they act inspired and desirous to bring them to fruition. They seemingly have the details worked out, and yet they never seem to get anywhere with their projects. It is their lot in this world to lose credibility with others. You know who they are. They announce grand plans to develop some great project or other, and the next time you see them they have moved on to the next big scheme. Expectation is the absolute ingredient for the fruition of any manifestation derived from the creative process of the individual. Expectation motivates people to preserve and stick through to

the end. Expectation is the trigger to manifesting anything and everything, from material possessions and artistic pursuits to the conditions in our lives. Period.

In reviewing the five laws, you may disagree. You may think of an example where you say to yourself, "All of the defined laws were in place in the project, and I truly believed that I would manifest it, but it still didn't happen." Well, if you really think that you defined and visualized the end product and that you were absolutely desirous and inspired, then I would estimate that your belief was not thorough or complete. In describing expectation, I mean that it is more an act of knowing than believing. Let me point out the differences.

It is important to become cognizant of the vast differences between knowing, believing, hoping, wishing, and dreaming. The act of knowing equates with a possession of facts, an awareness of or a surety about information. Knowingness is many times a result of experience. Knowing equates with a feeling as if you have already experienced the outcome.

Now let us ponder the term "belief." According to *Webster's New World Dictionary* (2003), belief equates to trust, confidence, faith, and opinion, or the conviction that certain things are true. Notice the lack of the association with fact. Our beliefs can likely be based on facts, but we are most likely to utilize the term knowledge in relation to hard facts. Most of us use the term "I believe" when describing our perception of how things operate in order to not offend another's belief. When we espouse beliefs, we can be varied in what we mean. We could be saying that we are merely open to the possibilities, as in "I believe that there is a God" or "I believe that a heaven exists."

Now think of the varying grade of intentions that can denote expectation. Let me use the example of someone who is contemplating purchasing a house. There are people who dream about one day owning a house, and there are folks who wish they could buy a house. Then there are those who espouse the hope of eventually buying a house. After dreaming, wishing, and hoping, we get down to the nitty-gritty: people who believe that they will buy a house. These folks will very likely buy a house, in time—some day, even after possibly being turned down on a mortgage or needing first to up their income. But if you say, "I believe I'll buy a house," it doesn't really carry the same weight of knowing.

Knowing is an absolute affirmation and decree to the world and yourself that you would utter with a statement like, "I am buying a house next month." Your intention is clear, real, and focused, and your expectation is undeniable.

It is my theory that the five laws of creativity have been the building blocks to every piece of matter and experiential condition that exists in the universe. They are an integral part of every manifestation of your own life and of my life. As I have stated, we are creating all of our experiences, conditions, and material manifestations 24/7, and each of these manifestations is subject to the laws—even if you don't realize it. That's because we are thinking close to 60,000 thoughts every day, and 95 percent of those thoughts are the same thoughts that we thought yesterday and the day before. Thus, our lives don't change much, we don't see much difference, and we don't realize the creative control that we have in everything we experience and manifest.

Whatever material conditions we feel most emotional about, and those that we truly expect to happen in our lives, come to fruition every day right there in front of us. Once we become aware of our thoughts, emotions, desires, visualizations, and expectations, we can harness them to create absolutely any material thing or condition that we can envision. Whether you are an artist, writer, musician, designer, performer, accountant, construction worker, or teacher, the active administration of these five elemental laws will bring you success at every measure. Every profession or skill has its own artistic nature and a variable outcome.

I believe that the Divine Artist of the Universe employs this same formula in the act of what we call creation. It is my belief that the Divine Artist conceived, blueprinted, inspired, desired, and expected all of what we know of as the universe, then triggered that expectation in one massive Big Bang. You might find that the concepts of each resulting material item, from the trillions of planets expanding outward to the cloud formations, mountainous landscapes, and the flora and fauna we know on Earth are not only amazing creations, but ever-expanding, evolving pieces of mind-formed matter.

Why do you think that we humans are so moved when we contemplate the stunning architecture and artistic nature of our natural surroundings? Well, if you see yourself in the shoes of such a creative master who could sculpt, paint, and form not only the beauty of the sunset upon the sea, but the smell of the air, and the sound of seagulls and ocean waves lapping in unison, what would be the one thing missing in this panorama of creation? Why, what every artist desires: recognition and appreciation.

That's where we come in. I believe that the Divine Artist created us to appreciate his work and to carry it on in our lives every day through the five laws of manifestation. If you haven't yet tried the formula, wait until you see how powerful the laws are. As you manifest the Wizard within, you'll harness them to create radical positive changes in your life and wield them with a powerful focus to create great works of vibrant art.

The Language of a Free Soul

Reverend Susanna Weiss

You're full of it. What is difficult to accept about creativity is the same as what is difficult to accept about spirituality: Each of us is full of the stuff. We are all filled with endless wells of creativity, just as we possess a limitless source of wisdom, goodness, and spirituality. Hard to believe, right? Those two qualities, creativity and spirituality, can seem so "other," so out there, so belonging to other people, not us. Yet the truth is that they are both available for the asking, and that we already possess them—there is an endless reserve in each of us. Just as we all have different innate talents and personalities, our creativity manifests in myriad ways. We each need to find our own way to enter into this inner source. But we all have those pools of creativity and spirituality within us, and they open the door to one another.

Of course, spirituality and creativity have many definitions, and they might both fall best into the category of pornography when it comes to identifying them. As Justice Potter Stewart famously said about pornography, "I know it when I see it." We know the feeling of spirit, the whisper of creativity when we feel it—those human attributes that have nothing to do with material values and pursuits. They lie in the realm of the heart that's not about physically living in the world, but in celebrating its beauty and ultimate meaning, the breathless excitement of experiencing intangibles.

We'll never touch them playing it safe, living only in what's comfortable and sure. It takes risk and willingness to shake things up, to wander about feeling uncertain, even lost and anxious. Creativity and spirituality happen on the edge, wedded together in an inner place often tapped best when challenged with uncertainty. I read an interview with a young Russian pianist who began as a child prodigy. He was a confident, powerful young man who seemed to possess an elegant ease about his talents and his ability to create. But when asked if he was ever nervous performing, he answered, "Always, so nervous that I can't eat or even drink anything. But that nervousness is really important, because as soon as I start playing the piano, it transforms into inspiration."

He described exactly my experiences of being a professional dancer for 25 years—the process of feeling nervous, edgy, perhaps even slightly ill while waiting in the wings; the stage lights, the music, waiting for my cue—feeling on an unbearable edge. But then, I would start dancing anyway and the nervousness would become an incredible energy that I could use to be at my best. A modern dancer is always interpreting the choreography, using body and soul to express both humanity and the sublime through the choreographer's steps. That creative process is never more present and vibrant than in performance, when uncertainty and undiscovered possibilities are brilliant cliffs to leap off. This leap takes us out of the usual world and opens up places within us that harbor a joy and connection with the essence of life. The creative leap lands us in the realm of inspiration, of spirituality. I have never felt closer to the divine than when I am dancing.

Even a still photograph that accompanied the interview with the Russian pianist conveyed the sense of sublime mystery in which he was participating. He was traveling on a path that bypasses thinking and logic, one that springs from what is simultaneously human and eternal inside each of us. It embodies the essence of feelings, a way to describe something unknowable and ultimately inexpressible. It's a journey that leads us to the eternal mysteries that transcend words and explanations.

Five years ago I co-founded with my husband a spiritual community in New York City, a place for each individual to explore and create their own spiritual path, not simply to accept and follow religious dogma laid down before by others. Why in the world at age 52 would I start such a thing? I had a long successful career as a dancer, still performing now and then, and was active in the company I founded, designing individualized, extended programs for clients to help resolve their physical problems. These might be orthopedic injuries, chronic pain, or conditions for which there is no helpful medical treatment. This work constantly challenged my creativity—needing to discover the ways to facilitate each individual's healing, not just replicate methods out of a textbook.

I had also been ordained an Interfaith minister, finding for the first time in my life a way onto many spiritual paths that touched my soul, and was happy performing weddings and exploring the wisdom and teachings that had been opened to me. However, I had never found a tradition where I could celebrate the sacred in a way that was meaningful to me—so I co-founded a spiritual community. Not a church, not a mosque, or a temple, but a place to gather with other seekers, and each discover our own spiritual path.

It has been a tremendous challenge. I'm ready to quit just about every week, but, somehow, creating on the edge where I have so many lessons to learn and am constantly challenged to find new depths and possibilities in myself has been worth it. It's the gift that uncertainty brings, the rewards—and the crashes—that await me as I regularly leap off that cliff.

To approach these mysteries we must have what is known as beginner's mind. Expectations and certainty—*knowing*—can be the greatest blocks both to creativity and spirituality. If we rely on expectations, all we can create is what we already know, or think we know, or would like to know, but the greatest creative part of each of us is yet to be discovered. Since embracing our spirituality acknowledges a part of self greater than what we know in our everyday world, that embrace opens us to our creative selves, to the part that has the possibility of creating something far beyond what we could ever imagine in this moment.

We might be highly respected accomplished experts in any number of fields, but studies and techniques can only help us to express the voice that comes from within—they can't be the source of it. All the knowledge we can acquire, all the skills we can hone are simply keys for unlocking the creativity within. Study allows our instincts to flow freely. They become the cliff from which we can take a step into the unknown and teeter on the edge where we are uncertain, a place where we feel we're journeying to places we've never before visited.

Undoubtedly, we'll make mistakes. We'll embarrass ourselves. If we're dancers, we'll fall, if we're writers, we'll get bad reviews, and if we're lucky enough to be as talented a composer as Stravinsky, Puccini, or Wagner, we'll be booed. If we're not willing to take those risks, creation won't happen on any meaningful level.

Spirituality and creativity, first and foremost, are not about how they look on the outside. They are an inner journey that we may share with others, or not. They are the language of a free soul. It is not a coincidence that dictators and autocratic societies suppress religious and artistic expression. As creative, spiritual beings we need to follow the classic advice: Give full effort, then let go of results. Focusing only on the end result inhibits us and can cause us to stumble on the journey of getting there. The journey is where the richness and joy truly happen.

The depth and importance of a creative or spiritual experience has little to do with the ultimate product. Whether it culminates in a profound spiritual awakening or in a breathtaking work of art doesn't change its effect on our inner life. The ephemeral moments of creating, imagining, soaring with an open heart are great jewels in our human experience. It doesn't matter whether or not we have the talents to write a violin sonata or offer profound poetry.

Even the most sublimely transcendent spiritual experiences are gently brushed into place by the great teachers. When breathless reports of our soaring states of meditation are offered to the master, the famous reply is, "Um hmm, ah yes, well, it will pass. Now, go back to your meditation cushion."

Another misconception that can stop the flow of our innate talents is that creativity is about what is presented to the audience. Because music, dance, theater, arts, books, paintings are all presented to be viewed, it's often assumed that it's the presentation that makes them creative. But that is the moment when the experience of creativity lies with the beholders. We all know the sensation of hearing a piece of music, seeing a dance, or reading an exquisite poem seemingly bypass any "brain" circuitry and go right to the soul. We are moved and touched and resonate with a human experience without having to think about it, intellectualize, or even understand the process. That is when a work of art becomes an experience of creativity for the audience, not the maker.

The audience's experience might be totally different from the creator's. Indeed, a public sharing isn't even necessary. A work of art may never be seen by anyone except the creator without diminishing its true value—and it certainly does not diminish the value of the creator's experience. Unlocking rich places in the heart while writing in a private journal, expressing the depth of emotions that can't be put into words through a painting that will never be exhibited, or a private dance that that is gone the moment it is danced are as precious to the creator as a celebrated and applauded public work of art.

Once we drop the idea that creativity needs to be presented to others to be of value, we can open to the joy of everyday creativity. Like true spirituality, there is no division between the inner and outer world. There aren't two boxes where we sort life into the sacred and the profane. There is no need for a temple or church, nor a need for a theatre or gallery. The creativity of the everyday can be the most enriching because it touches our lives where we live them, in the love and care that can be integral to the most ordinary daily need. Cooking is one of the best examples—even cooking a simple meal just for myself can be an experience of imagination and satisfying creation.

And what about the secret fear that others might have the stuff that it takes to be creative, but not me? This is the time to trust, to drop the bludgeon of self-judgment. Comparison with others has nothing to do with the value of the creative process. The perceived quality of whatever is created doesn't change in any way the value of the experience of creation—unless we let it. Every performing artist has had the disheartening experience of reading a "bad" review about their work, or at least one written by a reviewer who seemed to be at a different performance than they were. Suddenly as the words come from on high (especially awful if it's the *New York Times*) we are changed in our own view of the performance.

As a dancer, when my performance is over, it's finished: never to be edited, improved, or danced exactly that way ever again. No review, whether a rave or a pan, can change what happened. It can only affect our perception of what we've done; yet most of us are vulnerable to that. We don't even need the *Times* reviewer to do it. We accomplish it by ourselves with harsh self-criticism. If ever there is a time to leave that judging self out, it's when we are opening to the inner world of spirit and creation. At its ideal, it is a process without good or bad, no judgments, no reviews, just experience. Nothing inhibits creativity more than critical evaluation, nothing squelches its flow like ruthless self-editing.

As humans, we seek to know the part of ourselves that is eternal. We want to be in touch with the deepest meanings of why we are alive, how we fit into the scope of the universe, and know that we matter—that what we do has a meaning that can perhaps survive beyond our death. Connecting with that sense of eternity is found on the paths of both spirituality and creativity. They don't necessarily hold answers to

The Language of a Free Soul 91

the great mysteries that we ponder, but they ground us so that we can keep living and growing even with unanswered questions.

Since the creative process and our spiritual selves are beyond the material world, as we practice them we touch a wisdom and peace and excitement unavailable in our daily ordinary existence. This process isn't about talent, about how well we can play the cello, or not at all, or how exquisitely we sing, or not all. It's about our willingness to partake in the journey, our willingness to risk and open ourselves. These are the steps that allow us to connect with the eternal, which isn't necessarily grand and visible to the public. They can be private acts of creativity, small and ephemeral but no less powerful in opening to the part of our humanness that is also divine.

While this process happens privately, as an intimate journey that we take into the deepest center of ourselves, it's also where we can most exquisitely connect to others and offer them our gifts. We share our vision of the intangible beauty of existence that makes life worth living, and that helps us through hard times and eases the inevitable pain of living in this world. Touching others in this way affirms a truth that so easily gets lost in the shadows as we go about our everyday lives—the truth that we are all connected; deeply, eternally. Through creative experiences, we communicate on a level that strengthens that bond, the silent undercurrent of oneness that is the ground of our being. Creativity and spirituality are the languages of that bond, the means through which we can transcend outer differences, fears, prejudices, and separations, and feel our place as one connected soul. They enable us to leap over the boundaries of the material world—of our bodies—and express the joy and peace of interconnectedness.

The greatest gift that participating in creativity and spiritual exploration offers is the opening of the heart. Like other great and noble human experiences, such as love and generosity, they magically cause our innermost being to expand, to unclench, and to cross us over to understanding what is truly important in life. The tightness that can settle around our spirits, the knot of tension that constricts our center as we navigate the rush and pressure of modern life can be eased. Creativity is a respite from those pressures; spirituality is a refuge. When we lose touch with the joy of simply being alive as the demands of work or difficulties in relationships overwhelm us, creativity and spirituality can rescue us. They offer a breath of hope and tranquility that helps us to deal, to rest in the place of inner peace that is our birthright.

> *"It is the supreme art of the teacher to awaken joy in creative expression and knowledge."*
> —Albert Einstein (1879–1955),
> American physicist

Mapping Dreams, Creating Reality

Paige Stapleton

Humans are always creating. We begin creating the moment we have our first waking thoughts of how the day may go, as we are getting up. Then we dialogue with life all day. Sometimes we like the conversation, other times we don't. Having endured many years of frustration about my own conversation with life, several years ago I decided it was time to change my tactics. I wanted to know, "If my thoughts are creating my reality, how can I change what I think? How do I finally begin to create the life of my dreams?"

Since then I've discovered many thought-impacting tools that have helped me answer these questions. One of the most exciting, fun, and powerful is Life Mapping. Its purpose is to explore your subconscious to find out what is trying to emerge and become visible in your life. You create a Life Map by going through magazines and catalogues and cutting out anything that moves you: phrases and words that seem resonant; images that make you exclaim, "Ahhh . . . that's it! That's what I want my life to look like!" You then paste them onto a large piece of poster board in a way that makes sense to you. Afterwards, you display the Life Map where these items can continue to inspire and motivate you—and they gradually change what you focus your thoughts on.

I created my first Life Map in a seminar on abundance. Over 60 people who barely knew each other were seated in a huge room together. The trainers instructed us to create our "perfect life" by making a collage of things that represented what we wanted to see in our lives. We could concentrate on any area we wished: family, career, spirituality, home, health, or all of the above. The trainers said that when we were finished we would have the equivalent of our dreams in the palm of our hands. Then they let us loose with magazines, scissors, glue, ink stamps, stickers, and large pieces of poster board.

I remember feeling a bit intimidated at first. But pretty soon we were all ooohing and ahhhing, and snipping and sticking, and even yelling across the room for images we were specifically looking for. "Anybody see a baseball player . . . a guitar . . . a beach scene . . . a tree house?" We were tossing around magazines, pictures, glue sticks, and magic markers like rowdy kindergarteners. It was great fun letting our imaginations wander, having the freedom to consider any possibility, and then cutting it out and claiming it as something we could actually create in our own lives.

Before I started my Life Map that day, I took a few minutes to think about my dreams and what I wanted to see happen in my life. Recently, I'd been dreaming about putting together a multicultural concert, filled with talented, open-minded musicians. I saw people dancing and singing, lots of food tables and vendors, and people enjoying the sights, the sounds, and each other no matter what their background. I already had a name for it: Healing in Harmony.

Mapping Dreams, Creating Reality

As my Life Map began to take shape, I watched as a single picture of an Indian band grew into a montage of musicians that ranged from Indian singers to African drummers, to blues guitar players, to a didgeridoo player. I found images of people dancing in beautiful saris and tie-dyed shirts and added those to my collage. There was a party going on in my map—and it was my concert!

Then, I found a stunning picture of Heather Graham in a divine orange dress, a martini in her hand, surrounded by an entourage of people and grinning from ear to ear. I didn't want to be *her*, but I wanted to feel like she looked: beautiful, confident, supported, and in the absolute middle of her joy! So I placed Heather in the center of my Life Map to represent my desire to feel joy and exhilaration.

My heart started racing and I began to feel like the dream was already happening.

I decided, "Why stop there? How about love?" So I began searching through the magazine pages for an image of that perfect man—you know, the quintessential hottie! What I ultimately found that moved me most was a serene picture of St. Francis, the lover of nature, surrounded by birds and animals. As I gazed at it, I realized that he had the qualities I wanted in a man: quiet confidence, friendship with all creatures, and devotion to the Divine. I cut him out and glued him to my Life Map near Heather. Just to spice it up, I added a big red heart and the phrase "Best Sex Ever!" Okay, I was done.

My Life Map Becoming Reality

I took my map home with me and taped it on the wall of my apartment. There it was every day, a constant reminder of what I wanted to create in my life. I didn't make a point to look at it or study it. It was just there, sharing my space with me. Then . . . things began to happen. Out of the blue, I received a call from a friend, who said, "I have been thinking about your ideas for your concert, and I may have the perfect person for you to talk with." The next thing I knew, I was meeting people, sharing ideas, formulating plans, and creating the concert of my dreams, which ultimately took on the name Jam4Peace. It turned out to be a wonderful collaboration with two non-profit groups committed to raising awareness of compassionate communication and celebrating the beautiful diversity of our communities. We had musicians, belly dancers, speakers, a lovely spread of ethnic food, and a silent auction. People from all walks of life were dancing in the aisles and celebrating life together. Needless to say, the event was magnificent.

Not only was the event a success, my "St. Francis Man" was not far behind. A few months after the concert, I had my first date with the man who turned out to be the love of my life! I got to know him when he was helping me get my concert off the ground. He is a great lover of life, nature, animals, and ME. Yes, it was as though my entire vision had jumped off of the page and into my world.

Those Who Can't Do . . . Teach?

My next attempt to map my destiny didn't go quite as smoothly. Several months later I was again feeling an urge to get something moving in my life, but as I sat in my apartment looking through a multitude of publications and cutting out inspiring phrases and images, I just couldn't seem to put a Life Map together. I kept rearranging the words and images on my poster board, yet never seemed to get to the actual gluing part. Clearly I needed some support. I thought back on my original abundance class where I'd learned to do this activity and realized there had been something powerful about doing it with other people. I found myself wishing I could take another class to help me finish my new map. But there were no classes in Life Mapping that I knew of, so . . . I created my own class—and taught it!

The closest I had ever come to teaching was facilitating a support group for artists. But succeeding in this process was important to me, so I spoke with the minister of my church and proposed that I start a Life Mapping class to complement a class that she was teaching on principles of abundance. She thought it was a great idea.

I had no idea what kind of teacher I would be, or even if anyone would show up to take the class. And just before class started, I wanted to bolt out the door and never come back. But I took a few deep breaths and reminded myself, "All I am doing is sharing something that changed my own life. I can do this." I was shocked and thrilled when over 30 people eagerly walked through the door! I thought, "Wow, people are really interested in this and they clearly want some support around it, just like me."

I began by explaining what a Life Map is and sharing my past experience with them. Then I guided the class through a meditation, accompanied by live drumming and recorded flute music. I had never led a guided meditation, but somehow the words just flowed and when it was over, I could feel openness and willingness among the people in the room. We did a brief writing exercise, and then it was time to PLAY.

I had asked the students to bring their own magazines to add to the ones that I was providing. We spread them all out in a large pile in the middle of the room. We also had plenty of blank paper, markers, crayons, glitter, paint, stickers, scissors, and glue. Each student chose a few magazines to search through, and an intense hush fell over the room. Everyone was highly focused in their hunt for the perfect images and phrases for their maps. The mood seemed a bit too serious, so I added a little fun background music to lighten things up. And I began walking around the classroom, sharing in the excitement people were feeling when they found the ideal picture or the perfect phrase. I could feel the energy heighten as images that formerly had been trapped inside their minds came out, becoming something real on the once-blank sheets of paper.

One man used crayons to draw a huge audience that was focused on a picture of a dazzling dancer springing across the stage. Another was cutting out fantastic images of his dream home. A woman was covering all areas of her life and connecting them with stickers and streams of glitter. Each map was unique and personal. I literally was watching as people's desires became clearer to them. And the clearer they became, the more the students believed their dreams could be, and would be, accomplished. It was a privilege to witness the hopes and dreams of my students being revealed. Ideas were now visible on the page and had the potential to become reality.

A few weeks after the class, I heard from some of the students who wanted to share their progress. One woman had taken a long-awaited trip to Montana as a result of creating her Life Map. She was able to connect with some friends she had been talking with for years about starting a camp there to help women connect with themselves and others. Another woman framed her Life Map and called it her masterpiece. When some visitors to her home had asked her, "What is that?" she told them, "That's my life!"

Still another student shared that she had created a beautiful Relationship Map, full of couples and romantic scenes about love and partnership. She'd placed it on her door so she would see it every time she left her apartment. As time went on, she noticed that she felt angry each time she reached for the doorknob to leave. Her map was showing her that she was actually resistant to a relationship. She'd discovered it was time to explore what was blocking her from creating and having the love she desired in her life.

Third Time's the Charm

Although my class seemed helpful to everyone who took it, as the instructor I was so busy that I was unable to sit down and make a map. But after sharing in the excitement and breakthrough realizations of the participants, I was more determined than ever to pull my visions out of my head and get them down on paper. The next weekend, I finally set out to create my own Life Map with my boyfriend, Brian (aka, St. Francis), who was also interested in doing his own map. I never guessed what I would discover in this, now my third attempt at creating a new Life Map.

For most of my life I have been a singer with a deep love of music. I was sure that I wanted lots of references on my map to songwriting, guitar playing, and piano, and, naturally, singing. I went to the bookstore and bought nearly 50 dollars worth of magazines specific to music and songwriting. As I looked through my magazines, anticipating being moved and inspired by all of the musical images and phrases they contained, I found myself feeling just the opposite. I flipped through the pages continually thinking, "No . . . Ummm . . . No, I really don't want to go out on tour. Well, that isn't really it either . . . Uh no, I don't want to struggle with the other million singer-songwriters who never make a dime. No, not exactly what I want my days to look like, sitting in my room alone, practicing guitar and vocal scales."

While my pessimism and rejection of my lifelong dream was taking place inside me, Brian was seated next to me, as if in another world, clipping away one gorgeous, stunning picture and moving phrase after the other. His eyes were shining, he was grinning and laughing at his map that was developing, while I was ready to chuck it all and have a shot of tequila!

What was happening? I had been pursuing music since I could remember. Why couldn't I find one thing in these music magazines that represented my dreams?

Fortunately, Brian dragged himself out of his bliss long enough to notice that I was struggling and becoming very frustrated—even panicked. He suggested we take the dog for a walk, get some fresh air, and clear our heads. As we were walking and talking through how I was feeling, all of a sudden it hit me like a Mack truck, "That isn't my dream anymore! To focus on songwriting and singing just isn't where my heart is right now. Not that it may not be part of my life later on, but right now, it isn't where I want to put my energy." It was a HUGE revelation and the point when I realized how much Life Maps can show us not only about what our true desires are, but also about what former desires are no longer alive for us. We change, our dreams change, and so must our focus.

We walked home and I went back to my new Life Map with a new perspective, one that was open, fresh, uninhibited, and unlimited in possibilities. I found pictures of gorgeous mountain scenes, sunsets, amazing outdoor views from stunning living rooms and kitchens that attracted me, and the phrases, "Life is beautiful," "Just play," "Break the cycle," "Unleash Creativity," "Purpose revealed," "My Joy," and "Euphoria—live the dream!"

Shortly after completing that particular Life Map, Brian and I were offered a beautiful home in the Catskill Mountains in exchange for contributing a few hours a week as volunteers for the county historical society. Our living room had a picture window that overlooked a majestic mountain range, and every day we lived there we were blessed with a stunning display of sunrises, sunsets, and ever-changing clouds that surpassed any picture I had on my Life Map. Upon moving I was able to quit an uninspiring job at a bank. Since then every day is a day of creativity and play. My work feeds my spirit and brings me great joy.

Every morning I now do a mini-Life Map. I cut out a gorgeous, inspiring picture and a motivational phrase and paste them in my journal before I begin writing my morning pages. This reminds me of the power I have inside me to create the life of my deepest desires and greatest dreams. These maps can show us what we want, what we do not want, and what stands in the way of the fulfillment of our desires. I plan to continue to use Life Mapping as a way to stay in conversation with the unknowable force that resides in and around everything and everyone.

Ten Guaranteed Ways to Stifle Creativity

Kim Marcille

Perhaps you're tired of hearing about the benefits of creativity. You need an answer and you need it now! What good will it do you to muddle about in the artsy-fartsy world of creativity when you should be making plans, running numbers, and getting results? And particularly since you may not be feeling like the creative sort yourself . . . or at least, right at the moment. You're fresh out of ideas.

Hear, hear. That's what I say. There's been a lot of fuss about creativity and its value, and blah, blah, blah, but I'm with you: If I can't see it, if I can't touch it, if it's pie-in-the-sky dreaming, what possible use could it be? Imagine all that wasted time crafting a vision. You've got work to do!

Well, not to worry. It's easy to stifle creativity, if you know how. Just follow these ten easy steps, and every possibility that might arise will be crushed like a bug beneath your unrelenting boot of indifference.

1. ***Don't think about what you want.*** Certainly don't think about it in excruciating detail. Who cares what you want anyway? Don't you live and breathe to meet the needs of others? Thinking about what *you* want is just plain selfish—and there are plenty of people around you who are willing to tell you so. Avoid the whole bother by thinking mostly about what others expect of you. Spend all of your time trying to get into other people's heads and imagine how you could disappoint them or make them happy. That would be the safe thing to do.
2. ***Don't choose anything in particular for yourself.*** Choice is so . . . final. Once you've chosen an outcome, something you really want, there's that whole "commitment" thing to cope with. You've got to keep on wanting it, keep on maintaining your desire for it, and keep on honoring your decision to pursue it. Feh! So much

work, all that keeping on. Well, not actual work, just—you know—sort of a mindset. But isn't it easier not to set your mind on anything? Let it be brain-loose and fancy-free, instead of adding your own desires to the pile of desires you're already trying to fulfill for others. I mean, how much brains have you got, anyhow?

3. **Don't ask for anyone's guidance; particularly not someone you admire.** Those people you admire, they're all working much harder than you. It's true! You know it and I know it. They couldn't possibly be expending all that energy just to create something for which they have passion. They couldn't possibly be having the time of their lives doing it. If you ask them, you know they're just going to tell you to go for it, with all their "Go for it" bravado. Easy for them to say, now that they've already done it! But what about you? Wouldn't it be easier just to leave things as they are and go for a drink in the pub? Maybe you could invite someone you admire for a drink instead of asking for advice or support.

4. **Don't believe in any sort of dream.** Really. How naïve are you? Just because there are hundreds of thousands of people on the planet Earth today living their dreams doesn't remotely mean that you'll be one of them. The odds are like winning the lottery, aren't they? You know what makes those odds so high? The fact that people like you have a hard time maintaining their beliefs. You don't know how. You're not sure you even believe in your ability to manage your beliefs. And you're probably right. Just because your beliefs

produce amazing positive or negative effects in your body is no reason for you to begin caring about them. Don't try to pin your beliefs down as to whether they serve you or not. Don't try to create beliefs that would actually support you. Ignore them like most people do and, guaranteed, you'll stay on an even keel.

5. ***Don't tell anyone about your dream.*** God forbid they should tell anyone else! Next thing you know, perfect strangers at parties will begin to ask about your dream. They'll want to know if it's "done" yet, as if it were a batch of cookies. What right have they got to know? Let's be clear right now: Your dream is your dirty little secret. If you let it out, others will try to encourage you to make it come true. Who needs that kind of motivation? Gosh, if others started to invest in your dream, then who knows *what* could happen: resources and coincidences popping up out of nowhere! Like you need that sort of *falderal* in your life. Bah, humbug.

6. ***Worry more.*** Everyone knows that life is struggle and strife until you die. If you were meant to have fun, God would have made the whole world Disneyland, wouldn't he? Instead, you've got bills to pay and kids to feed, and parents to take care of, and lots and lots of other things to worry about daily. You'd like to stop worrying, but we all know that worry makes the world go 'round. Even if 99 percent of what you worry about never comes true, aren't you happy knowing that you're prepared for that bastardly 1 percent? Without worry, you'd be nowhere. Imagine all those extra

brain cells you'd recoup and have to repurpose. Like you have time to figure *that* out.

7. **Don't think about your options.** Don't think about what your life might be like if you suddenly started doing something you enjoy. What a waste of energy that is! Much easier to assume that your fate is pre-determined and just ride the track from here 'til the end. Oh, I suppose you *could* change the course of your life. But imagine all the wreckage you'll leave in your wake: friends who don't know who you are anymore, because you don't want to spend your time the same way as you used to; family members who think you're a fool for trying to improve your luck; a spouse who feels abandoned because your new "thing" is boring as hell to him or her. Whatever. You can't afford those kinds of losses. Trust me. You'll never make any new friends. Your family won't survive if you shift gears. Your spouse is probably already packing because you "look funny." Don't even think about the options. There aren't any. Stuck, stuck, stuck is the name of the game for you.

8. **Don't take any risks.** Play it safe. Nobody *really* cares about you but you. If you don't take care of yourself, who will? You can't be putting yourself out there day after day endangering the security you've spent all these years building up. You've got a comfort zone and you should stick to it. Sure, it's the size of a postage stamp, but so what? You don't really need to be braver, do you? If you were braver, you might do something foolish, like dart into a burning building to save some children or speak in public. I offer these

thoughts only in your best interest. If you don't challenge yourself, you have a much lower chance of getting hurt. Go with the obvious.
9. ***Take poorly timed measurements of your progress, and take them often.*** To really stifle creativity, be sure to measure your progress toward any creative goal at all the wrong times. Measure yourself when you haven't done a creative thing all day, all week, or all month. Write it down! You'll want to preserve these moments for posterity. Or, for high impact, take a measurement of your progress when you feel you've done something particularly stupid. If you're so dumb—and we know you are—you'll never achieve anything creative anyway. Be sure to capture these moments in all their detail to confirm your limited ability to do anything right. These records will help you get over yourself and any inclination to be creative. By now, you should be feeling even the slightest remaining wisp of your creative ideas blowing away on the wind.
10. ***Don't even think the words "vision," "dream," "possibility," or "creativity."*** The less you open your mind to the thought that unlimited possibility exists in the universe and that you just might be able to access it, the better off you'll be. The absolute evil here is practicing the visioning process that people are talking so much about these days. Because the more you practice, the better you'll be at it, and then creativity will enter your life whether you want it or not. You may even discover that you are the creator of your experience, and then what will we

have accomplished? Don't embarrass either of us. Accept your lot, leave well enough alone, and you'll find your creativity leached out of you like the life-as-you-know-it endangering disease that it is.

I hope that you've found these tips useful in your endeavor to stifle creativity. If, on the other hand, you've found these tips an inspiration to perhaps give creativity a go, well, I wish you luck my friend. You'll probably change your life and get what you want.
Don't say I didn't warn you.

Are You Pregnant?
Five Ways to Get That Labor Over Quickly and Give Birth to Your Possibilities

Sandy Grason

I was having a chat with one of my clients last week, and she told me she's been procrastinating about her business lately. Chris is juggling lots of different things right now. She is working full time at a corporate job she finds very stressful, and she is working part-time on her passion. She plans to make her part-time business a full-time business as soon as she can, but several things are holding her back: lack of money, lack of time, and lots of fear.

Can anybody out there relate to Chris? I sure can!

Are You Pregnant? 109

- Do you feel like you're juggling an insanely high number of projects at the same time, including trying to have a personal life that's meaningful and makes a difference in the world?
- Do you have lots of really great ideas, but you have trouble putting them into action?
- How long have you been writing, speaking, and planning your dream life? Do you still feel like you're not much closer to realizing it?

Guess what? You're pregnant—pregnant with possibilities. Maybe you've just realized that you're pregnant. You are in the first trimester. Nobody else knows what's "cooking" inside of you, and you're not quite ready to share the news with the world. Maybe you are at the tail end of your second trimester. Everyone you meet asks you when you are due. When is this "baby" gonna get here? These questions make you excited, nervous, and a little uncertain about how you are going to "do it all."

Maybe you are in labor. The "baby" is done and ready to come into the world. It is time! But you are tired and worn out. You need some support to give birth to this amazing new possibility.

Giving birth to your creativity is very much like giving birth to a human child. The pregnant part of the process can last months, or even years. Unlike with the birth of a human child, where a doctor will induce labor if the baby has been growing inside of you for too long, unless you've got support in place for your creative projects, you could be pregnant forever and never actually give birth to the amazing possibilities growing inside of you.

I've given birth three times. Twice it resulted in an amazing little person who I share my life with. Once it resulted in an international revolution called The Journalution. Each time I went through long, strenuous months of developing, growing, and creating the magical possibility that was living inside of me. Each time there were also many, many moments when I felt lost and alone. I thought I was the only one in the world who ever felt this way.

All three times I said, "I can't do this. It's too hard. I don't know how anybody can go through this!" But when it was all over and I was holding that incredible, life-changing, living, breathing "baby" in my hands, I was so grateful that I did it. I was in awe of myself then. And I am still in awe of myself.

I want you to feel that way, too. You have a glimpse of possibility inside of you for a reason. You are meant to give birth to it—or you would not have been given the vision. Here are a few of the tools that have helped me move forward in my birthing process with ease, grace, and *speed*. Perhaps they will help you as well.

1. **Reconnect.** This is always the first step . . . No matter what's happening in your life, if you're feeling as if you are running in circles and not inspired, or as if you are so damn pregnant you can't get up off the couch, here's where you start. Breathe. Reconnect. I know, you've heard this a million times, but, seriously, you should be doing this every day! At least once a day.

    I don't particularly like rules, but here's one rule I try to follow. Every single day, I breathe. (Ha-ha.) I mean breathe deeply, with intention.

Your intention is to get back to that space of knowingness. It's there. I promise. Here's how to do it: Close your eyes and take a deep breath in through your nose, as deeply as you can. Hold the breath for just a moment, and then, very slowly, release the breath through your mouth. I do this three to five times to relax my body and get myself "back in my body."

What I mean by "in your head" is that if you are running around and checking things off of your to-do list, taking phone calls, answering emails, and generally responding to life's interruptions, doing the things that you absolutely have to get done in order to live in our society, you are showing a tendency to operate in your head.

When I'm in my head, I see my energy buzzing up above my head like bees: buzz, buzz, buzz. Those bees are busy up there, reminding me of all the things I forgot to do. "Don't forget this, don't forget that, what about that? What are you going to do about that?" When I take deep, intentional breaths, I visualize myself pulling that energy down through my neck and spine and into my heart. Like a straw, with each inhale I pull the energy down into my heart, my lungs, my belly, and then down into my lower body. I visualize that this breath is a beautiful white or golden light that runs up and down my spine, connecting me to something greater than myself and grounding me into the Earth at the same time.

With each exhalation I affirm that I am releasing anything that no longer serves me. This breathing will almost immediately reconnect me to

a still place inside of my body, a place where I can communicate with that part of me that is wise and powerful and has the answers I am seeking.
2. ***Give Your Self a Break.*** Many highly successful "go-getter" women tend to go-go-go-go and rarely stop to take a break. So when you're feeling a little overwhelmed and aren't sure what to do next, the very next thing you must do is stop. That's right. Stop what you are doing and take a break. When you move from one task to the next to the next, it doesn't matter how much you are accomplishing, you are only focused on "what's next." So stop, breathe, and congratulate yourself on all that you are doing today and all that you have done.

I call this my "Look What I Did List," and if you've never done one, do it now! Go back through your calendars, journals, and emails for the last year and make a list of your accomplishments. Allow yourself to write down every big and little thing that you've done in the last year. (If you've never done this before, you can go back as far as you like). If you are constantly moving from one goal to the next, you set yourself up for "When _____ happens, then I'll be happy." Only you never give yourself the opportunity to appreciate the _____.

When you celebrate your accomplishments, before moving on to the next goal or to-do item, you are starting from a place of "fullness." I want you to be full of yourself before you make another move on your project. This is where the real fulfillment will come in. You are already proud, full, and complete. The next project is just another

Are You Pregnant? 113

experience or dream you are bringing to life, not something to achieve in order to be happy.
3. ***Write Your Big Vision.*** Okay, so now you are beginning to feel relaxed and reconnected. You've created some space inside of yourself and congratulated yourself for all that you already do. You are ready to bring that possibility into the world. It all starts with a vision. I like to pick one big thing that you are working on or one great idea that you've had and then write about it as "A Perfect Day." Here's the way to do this exercise:

Imagine that you are getting ready for this "vision" and it's happening today or tomorrow morning. How would you be spending that day? When would you wake up? What would you eat for breakfast? What would your house look like? Who would be living or visiting in your house? Remember, we're talking "perfect day" here, no time to be realistic. Just get that really, big, scary, fun, exciting vision down on paper. (For more inspiration on creating your perfect day vision you can download journaling prompts at **www.sandygrason.com.** These audio tracks contain relaxing, reconnecting journaling instructions accompanied by soft music. Listening to one is like having a personal journaling session with me.) The important thing is to get your creativity flowing onto the blank page. No editing. For ten minutes, ignore the critical or doubting voices and allow yourself to write *anything*.
4. ***Share Your Big Vision.*** Now that you've got a working vision down on paper, go share it with someone. This is the power of the mastermind that

Napoleon Hill talks about. "Two or more gathered together creates miracles." A few guidelines here:
- Pick someone who will support you unconditionally in your greatest vision.
- Tell them before you read, "I want you to listen and tell me how fabulous I am. I'm not ready for feedback or brainstorming yet. I just want you to hold this vision for me."
- Read your Perfect Day vision to them exactly as you have it written.
- As you read your Perfect Day, notice if anything feels off. Change anything that doesn't give you an immediate feeling of "Yes!" You want this Perfect Day to energize you when you read it. Don't worry if you feel a little nervous or uncomfortable sharing this vision, you are supposed to feel this way. I tell my clients, "If you don't have those butterflies in your belly, you need to go get a bigger dream." Break out of your comfort zone and take a chance!

5. ***Take One Inspired Action.*** Read your vision every day, connect to the vision, and see yourself experiencing it right now. Put yourself in the room each day, feeling those feelings, and then ask yourself, "What one thing could I do today that would have the greatest impact toward drawing this vision into my life?" Notice the first thing that pops into your head. Just take a moment to notice. Try not to judge the idea. Write down the first thing that comes into your mind. Then go do it! Don't judge your idea. Don't worry about what that inspiration has to do with the big picture. Don't try to figure out what's going to happen next. Just go

do it. Now! This is where you begin to invite the magic into your life to play.

I've given birth a few more times since my first book *Journalution* was born. The process continues to fascinate me. In fact, as I write this, I'm laboring on two new projects. And yes, on some days it's hard and I feel like I want to give up. But if I ask myself, "Why am I doing this?" from deep within me comes a voice that says, "Because this is what you are meant to do in the world. You must be the greatest version of Sandy-licious that you can be."

You can choose to ignore those pregnancy pains and most likely you will never give birth to all of the amazing possibilities that are growing inside of you. If you sit back and stay comfortable, the world will never have the opportunity to experience your purpose. That would be a shame. I understand that sometimes it's hard and confusing. I know that there are many, many different directions you could go. If you follow the steps I've laid out for you, reconnect, give yourself time, write your vision, share your vision and take inspired action, then your creativity will flow through you into the world. The world is waiting for your magnificence.

It's time: Go be your fabulous, delicious self.

Want to Write Like Mozart?

Janet Conner

Wolfgang Amadeus Mozart lived long before anyone heard of brain waves. But he knew how to recognize and utilize the theta brain wave state that supports creativity. And you can, too. "Mozart?" I can hear you thinking. "Excuse me, but isn't this essay about writing? How can Mozart help me write?"

Well, I confess that Mozart was not the first person who came to mind when I thought about writing and writers. But then this Mozart quote landed in my inbox: "When I am, as it were, completely myself, entirely alone, and of good cheer—say traveling in a carriage, or walking after a good meal, or during the night when I cannot sleep—it is on such occasions that my ideas flow best, and most abundantly. Whence and how they come, I know not, nor can I force them."

I stared at the quote. I read it three times. I knew I'd just been handed the perfect way to teach you about the theta brain wave state. Mozart never heard of theta, but there's no doubt in my mind that that's exactly what he's describing. And theta is where we writers want to be.

Let me explain. There are four basic brain waves: beta, alpha, theta, and delta. Beta waves, the fastest, are associated with stress. When you awake abruptly to an alarm clock and immediately start focusing on all the things you have to do, you are leaping from the slowest delta brainwaves of sleep right into high-speed beta. Most of us live the bulk of our days in fast-paced beta. Alpha waves are a bit slower. You are in alpha when you concentrate and focus. You've heard people talk about being "in the zone." That's a deep alpha brain wave state.

Theta waves are slower still. You experience them briefly as you awaken. During those first drowsy moments, you can remember your dreams. In those precious seconds, you can also have truly creative ideas and breakthroughs. Have you ever awakened suddenly "knowing" the solution to a problem? That's theta. Brain scans of people who meditate show that they drop quickly into deeper and deeper layers of theta.

So what does this have to do with writing and creativity? Everything. One reason people think writing is hard work is that it is hard work if your brain is smoking along in high-speed beta. In beta mind, it's tough to hold your focus, and it is way too easy to get hung up on individual words instead of letting ideas flow. If you want to write a book that makes a difference in the world, you want to train yourself to enter and take advantage of the fabulous ideas available to you in the theta brain wave state.

Look back at what Mozart said: "When I am, as it were, completely myself, entirely alone, and of good cheer." There are two big clues here: alone and unstressed. Just as you can't meditate while talking with someone; you can't enter theta mind when you're talking. Be still. Be quiet. Be alone. That's fairly simple.

The stress piece is a little tougher. If I order you to stop being stressed, you'll actually become more stressed, because I've brought your level of stress into your conscious awareness. So here's a little trick: Breathe deeply and slowly, inhaling through your nose and exhaling through your mouth. It is a physiological impossibility to be stressed while breathing deeply. Every time you sit down to write, breathe.

What else did our boy genius say? "Traveling in a carriage, or walking after a good meal, or during the night when I cannot sleep." Have you had the experience of realizing, as you pull into a parking space, that you have no memory of driving, but you suddenly know how to handle something you've been worried about? Somewhere on that drive, you slipped into theta.

But what about Mozart's comment about not being able to sleep? Most of us view being awakened in the middle of the night as a bad thing. We start stressing over how soon the alarm is going to go off and how exhausted we're going to be. Of course, the more we worry, the more awake we are, and the whole miserable circle repeats until the alarm puts us out of our misery. But what if waking in the middle of the night is not a loss of sleep, but a gift of new ideas and solutions? Mozart said, "It is on such occasions that my ideas flow best, and most abundantly." Well, we writers want abundant flowing ideas, too.

When I was writing my book *Writing Down Your Soul*, I stumbled upon this information about theta brain waves. I thought it was the most exciting thing I'd heard. And it made so much sense. I've awakened many times in my life "knowing" what to do, but I never knew why that happened. Once I knew it was theta, I wanted to consciously use it. Mozart may have said, "Whence and how they come, I know not, nor can I force them," but I sure wanted to try. Here's what I did.

As I was falling asleep I told my subconscious mind what to work on while I was asleep. Then I drifted off with a notepad next to the bed. During the night I would be awakened several times. Each time, I'd roll over, write down what I "heard," whisper "Thank you," and go back to sleep. As I woke the next morning, I'd lie perfectly still, probing for the last vestiges of dreams and ideas. Finally, I'd sit up and write down everything I remembered. An hour later, when I went to my office, I'd look at my night notes and simply follow my "instructions" for the day.

This worked so well that I started placing orders. When the book was almost finished, I didn't like the ending, so I placed an order for a good ending. I actually said out loud, "I'm going to make dinner, would you please work on the ending? Thanks." Then I went downstairs, made chicken piccata and listened to Miles Davis. Around nine o'clock, I got this urge to pick up a notepad. I sat down immediately and out poured the ending. It felt more like taking dictation than writing. What was happening? Was theta mind taking over? Had my order been filled? I don't really know. All I know is I adore the last chapter in my book. When I read it, I think, "Wow, this is really good. Who wrote this?" And then I remember, "Oh, I did."

This is now my *modus operandi* for writing. I let my subconscious mind know what I'm working on and then I sleep on it. I request creative help on every writing and speaking project and, as far as I can tell, I always get it. I may not be in Mozart's league, but I can certainly play in theta mind. And so can you.

Inspiration, Desperation, and Curiosity Beget Creativity

Carol Hoenig

From the beginning of time, our forebears were discovering ways to survive while improving their quality of life, yet their spirits yearned for more than food for the belly and covering for the body. Along with the first hammer came the flute; with the first utterances, tunes. All through the ages, because of the human desire to know more, to leave one's mark, and to share how we see the world, creativity occurs. Usually, the very word *creativity* implies the world of art, music, dance, and literature. Yet, that is not necessarily the case. Creativity comes from the desire to reach beyond the ordinary, which could be fueled by desperation, greed, or a reaction to an injustice. Or even maybe something less obvious, as it was for me.

    I don't actually recall being taught to value creativity, unless I count the time when my first grade teacher, Mrs. Gadway, instructed my classmates and me how to behave prior to attending our first school concert. We weren't to talk while the orchestra performed, but we were to applaud in appreciation once each song concluded. I wasn't sure what to make of my teacher's stern instructions but looked forward to doing something out of the ordinary as my peers and I walked single file from the elementary wing of the school to the high school auditorium.

Before long, we were seated in the bleachers. I remained very still, not wanting to risk Mrs. Gadway catching me misbehaving and sending me back to the classroom. Moments later, the lush, green velvet curtain rose to reveal students posed with their instruments ready to perform. The conductor raised his baton and a hush came over the auditorium. Then it happened, at least for me. I became lost in the strings of the violins, my soul suddenly feeling free with possibility. I closed my eyes and was no longer in that room but someplace where I could be all that I was meant to be. I'm sure wrong notes were struck, but at such a young age, I only heard perfection. My reverie, however, was broken when a nearby classmate whispered loudly, "Look at Carol."

I felt the blood rush to my face as giggles confirmed I'd been caught escaping my small town existence through a newfound medium. Watchful students ready to laugh again at my far-away expression kept me from appreciating the rest of the concert. Fortunately, though, the mortified little girl I was had a taste of something so extraordinary that day that the embarrassment took a backseat to the idea of possibility.

It was just a high school band performing in a small school in upstate New York. Quite likely, few, if any, of the students in the orchestra went beyond high school in their musical education. We lived in a rural area where farming was the livelihood that didn't offer a terribly prosperous living. Still, there was one day in 1961 when one little girl was touched by a sound that galvanized her enough to make her want to express her own creativity.

The problem was that I didn't have a strong desire to play an instrument. Instead, it was as though the violin was playing me, moving me to create in my own way. But I was in first grade and had little idea just how to respond to the visceral longing. I'd pound out *Chopsticks* or *Heart and Soul* on my parents' untuned upright piano, and peck out something that resembled *Greensleeves*, but it didn't fill the void. Those songs didn't tell the stories that were churning, as churning as a child can feel, inside me.

Nighttime was my favorite time. I'd lie in bed in the dark, able to pretend I was far away from my bland existence, and quietly create an imaginative world where people lived exciting lives and spoke eloquently. Yet, by morning, I'd have to leave those people behind. But then I convinced my mother to give me the previous season's Sears & Roebuck catalog so that I could cut out the models—men, women, and children—in various poses, wearing the latest styles. These very original paper dolls covered my bedroom floor and were participants in the stories I made up. I didn't think I was being creative. Rather, it was more that I had to find a way to express myself while longing to escape my sepia-colored life. I suppose it was much the same way for our ancestors who needed to find an incentive far from the mundane.

Then, a couple of years later, when I was in third grade, my teacher introduced a thick book filled with poetry. At first daunting in appearance, the book soon became a welcoming sight. I looked forward to hearing the rhythmic sounds, as my teacher would read each day to the class. More exciting was the assignment to write our own poetry. It wasn't long before I discovered that poems weren't just for schoolbooks. Soon, I was neatly tucking humorous phrases between rhyming words, like *hat* and *cat* or *fly* and *cry*, on lined paper. The praise I received made me believe what I had to say was worth listening to. I still have those poems, the paper yellow with age, and it's obvious the praise was nothing more than kind gesture, yet it was enough to encourage me to continue.

As time went by, the improvised paper dolls vanished while my bedroom walls began to fill with sheets of paper displaying verses I'd tapped out on a Smith & Corona manual typewriter that my parents bought me for my eleventh birthday. I enjoyed cracking open books, but without access to a public library or bookstore when school closed for vacation, I had to rely on my own imagination for drama. I suppose one could consider my creativity was inspired by a young girl's desperation for wanting more.

One year followed the next, and I continued writing as a hobby, but tried my hand at other more sensible occupations, because one needs to eat. In between marriage, raising my children, and divorce, I had a number of jobs. I worked for a short time as an office manager, but quit only months later due to feeling unchallenged. Then, I took some design classes, thinking perhaps I'd enjoy being an interior decorator. After the first few classes, though, boredom set in once again. It was when I was sitting at my computer that I felt settled. It was clear that I was more fulfilled decorating homes within narrative dimensions instead of the real world. Besides, it was around this time that answers I thought were black and white began to gray. I needed to explore the questions that were suddenly becoming so intense they gave me little rest. Therefore, even though it took time and yielded no money, I began exploring these questions in the form of a novel. It was as though I had little choice.

Now, it was those questions and that desperate need for something out of the ordinary that has been the impetus for my source of revenue. Like the previously mentioned farmer, it doesn't offer a terribly prosperous living, but it does satisfy a hunger. There is a struggle, however, when I must force the writer within me to finish a deadline because the mortgage must be paid; I worry that the passion will be contrived and compromised. Then again, no matter what I have to do to pay the bills, I will always find a way to write. Being creative helps me understand the world in a way that I may not have been able to do otherwise.

I do wonder, though, what became of those classmates from first grade who embarrassed me? How is it that they weren't as enthralled by the music as I was? Why didn't it stir their creative juices, so to speak? Are their days simply ordinary? Maybe they were of the ilk that prefers a hammer to a flute. And that is okay, because the little girl sitting in those bleachers so long ago still managed to discover what was possible when that velvet curtain rose.

Creativity Rising

Maria Yraceburu

Storytelling is an ancient art wherein wisdom, skills, and entertainment are shared by letting words of power flow with the control and skill of a master time-weaver. Stories help us look back and plan ahead. I am such a storyteller and come from a long line of storytellers. This lineage, the oral traditions of the Quero Apache Tlish Diyan, my heritage, continues through me. This has come after years of traditional apprenticeship and by living in close communication and connection to the ancient earth wisdom I was blessed to receive.

The winds have called Kamaka Naakai Ts'ilsoose, or Hawkeye Returning Star, as I am known, born for the Red Paint People and given a charter of time. Because of the nature of my training, I know storytelling to be a fine art with a beginning, ending, intent, and a knack for casting choreographed words of power upon the ethers for listeners to interpret upon reception. Usually within a 12-hour period that follows hearing a story of this nature, the listener has a profound experience that often changes their lives. Those who are familiar with the art of traditional storytelling know that its method is vast, beautiful, and wastes no opportunity.

Whether I am preparing something for printed publication, a lecture, or a ceremonial enactment, the preparation is the same. In each, I apply various philosophical teachings, which have been abundantly provided through my life experiences. For this reason, I am confident in my expression of my spirit . . . my passion . . . my truth. My earthwalk is supported by integrity.

Every storyteller has his or her style in mingling historical reverence, presentation style, and ability to flow and ad lib in a sacred, beautiful, and profound manner. Plot and sequencing, and embellishment with wonderful life experience, involve listeners and readers. The Sacred Parents—Earth and Spirit—fashioned me as an information choreographer, a playful Little One, given the responsibility during my lifespan to share and impart understanding of earth, life, and spirit . . . earth, sky, animals, birds . . . with others. If there's an atom in motion, it's alive. With awareness, we unite traditions and come together so that each entity is relevant. Relationships are acts that transform ancient wisdom into new ways of doing things. They produce a type of quickening heart surge.

My creative preparations are done in a structured process that revolves around a ritual that can be done in one to nine days, depending on the task I am taking on. I believe I dream these things into being. Chants, prayers, these are my openings to inspiration. As are playing my flute or drum. Many other rituals bring visions of intent and detail. The sequence of my stories is choreographed for optimum potential. Listeners or readers must be able to feel a part of what is happening in the final effort. I've been told that my stories are universal teachings, their transitions are effective, their words beautifully integrative in nature, and I ponder the awakening hearts they touch. I honor listeners and readers for their participation.

Before creation, usually I do a detox for a couple of days if my endeavor is a book, painting, or ceremony. I purify my body by watching what I eat, removing myself from chaotic or negative situations, and I love myself, for I know this element brings me in touch with the magic of creative imagination. This dynamic regimen helps me create situations and experiences that heal, bless, instruct, renew, and open perception. It is a regimen that works for me, and one that cannot be rushed.

During my preparatory period, I receive visions of essential themes, character identities, relationship interchanges, and ritualistic actions, both ancient and contemporary. I witness the overlaying of time within my mind's eye. Each story component is received with reverence as I recognize the honor associated with my life purpose. To share the legends and ways of the earth is a way of receiving life in an expansive manner.

I present my stories in two different manners, those that are written and belong to the rhythm of the mind, and those presented in ceremonies as interactive, spontaneous plays belonging to the rhythm of the universe. Energy is different when engaging universal rhythm, so we, like All Our Relations, must receive and act differently. A story presented as a ritualistic interaction during ceremony is spontaneous, lasts a moment in duration, yet moves the heart spirit. There are no rewrites or edits. A written story can be ever-changing once committed to publication. Only, if the reader understands that interpretation, like ceremony, a story is always in the Now. If the written story is received new each time, each reading shall reveal something new. An experienced storyteller can relay infinite reality. Symbolically, the experience of the story involves becoming the very essence of sacred resolution, the very truth of the moment.

Stories and ceremonies have miraculous effects on people, for the healing power of a story shared is the unifying heart of commonality, of innocence. I believe deeply in the power of words that comes to me to bring understanding of my life. After I receive a story, I feel it in my body, radiating from my heart outward. A story is shot like a little arrow of thought into a consciousness of reality, which ripples into the waves of emotion.

Storytelling is one of the most beautiful and sacred rituals, and when I do it I give of myself with all that I am. The experience is a sense of honoring and trust. I consider it a privilege to share words that have been shared and dreamed. Life is the expressed dedication to honor.

I write. I tell a story . . . I prepare by doing and allowing space for creativity to flow . . . I squint my eyes against the sun, and reflect on the experiences that have brought me to fulfilling destiny. Much of it, especially in the middle years, was laced in shadow. It might have seemed like I'd lost my way. A Spirit Guide helped me through that. Young, lonely in the twilight . . . sometimes she seemed confused. Sometimes I would see her sleeping in a garden, her head propped up against a tree. She would recognize my presence. This was a dream that was not a dream, but moments of the future remembered.

I realized, of course, that my path had turned to the light when Toho'ma entered my life in waking reality. With tremendous support of my *housthe*-helpmate-life partner-twin flame, I knew that my Grandfather Ten Bears' prophecies for my life would come to pass. Grandfather insisted that I train in all aspects of our traditions. The aging Holy One passed on to me his lineage knowledge and the power of his love for life. The venom of the rattlesnake and the strike of the Thunder Beings later completed my initiations. An arrowhead necklace (the arrow of truth) carried me into guardianship of *Esonknhsendehi*, Changing Mother Earth.

I squirm a little these days when I connect to the sensation of the shifting magnetic earth grid. I pray for humanity to recognize its interconnection with the physical dynamics of world evolution. I hear others around me sigh and continue to believe in their isolation. They daintily avoid their power. I speak to them lovingly and affirm the truth of their essence.

Grandfather taught me only to affirm or give energy to the positive. This action has awakened me perhaps more than any other. "Unconditional love," he explained, "means no attachment." He loved me without expectation, supporting my positive potential even in my days of darkness. He was the finest man I ever met. Healings and holyway rituals of earth renewal along with stories describing the mysteries of the universe were his magic. Of humanity, Ten Bears was especially confident. Individually, he knew each essence.

Ten Bears ascended during life. He accomplished the connection between himself and All That Is. In his final act of power, he left me his evolutional legacy: a touch of light to instruct and guide.

I am a fortunate woman to be surrounded by awakening souls remembering themselves. I was fortunate enough to be Ten Bears' continuance. Although I had a moment of shadow—doubt veiled in illusion—the outcome surpasses my dreams: the Seven Worlds Prophecies.

A pattern develops. Push through years. Information is forthcoming, then more surely. It has become obvious to me as well as to others that a major world shift is upon us. Science has documented reversing magnetic poles, a decrease of ozone, increased tectonic plate movement, volcanic activity, and shifting weather patterns. Those who nod and point to spiritual integration as the reason, do so knowingly. Life requires continued respect and care.

Now we dream, our wildest expectations limited beside the real story that is unfolding.

> *"There is a vitality, a life force, an energy, a quickening, that is translated through you into action, and because there is only one of you in all time, this expression is unique."*
> —Martha Graham (1894-1991),
> American dancer and choreographer

Creating Your Ideal Life? It's Always Up to You

Howard Falco

"Don't ask yourself what the world needs. Ask yourself what makes you come alive and then go do that. Because what the world needs is people who have come alive."
—Howard Thurman

Take a deep breath and relax. Right now you are where you're supposed to be. You'll eventually discover that any thought to the contrary that surfaces in your mind is some form of denial or delusion. In reality, if you should have, or could have, done something differently in the past, you would have. All the previous choices you made and all the actions you took were necessary and perfect to get you to this exact moment, right here and now. The reason understanding this is so important is that if you do continue living in the past in your mind—examining and re-examining events that are over and gone—you are not actively and purposely creating your future. If you are stuck in an experience of past time, the reality you desire stays in an idea of the future.

The only way to act creatively so that you may have what you desire is to stay focused in the only time there ever is: the moment. In this state of mind, you are able to harness your immense power to create your life exactly as you imagine it could be.

Past the perceived limits in your mind, there is a space of understanding where all possibility exists. Time is irrelevant here, because everything here is the present moment. There is no past or future in this state of mind. It is a perspective from which a thought and its manifestation appear to be simultaneous. There is no thinking, only knowing; no fear, only faith; no resistance, only acceptance. Each time you have created something, you have done so by entering this harmonious, non-resistant *present* state of mind.

While much of your life has been created automatically on a subconscious level, you have begun to understand that you could take this process to the entirely conscious level by tapping into the state of presence. If this were not so, then you would not be reading these words. It is as if the universe is answering your questions with a big, flashing colored neon sign that reads: *You are in control.*

I wouldn't say I was uncreative before I saw my own "flashing neon sign," just that I wasn't aware I was in full charge of everything I created and experienced. I simply didn't realize the extent of the creative energy I was putting out to the world every day through my choices and actions. In addition, while my past choices seemed to come from an idea about myself that was unfulfilling to me, when I changed that self-concept my life changed.

Furthermore, I was able to accelerate the changes in my life once I realized that my self-concept is always and entirely up to me. In other words, who I was in the past does not have to be who I decide to be and create from in the present. Who I am now does not have to be who I am and create from in the future. At any moment I am free to declare myself anew and enjoy a different experience created from this fresh identity.

In my book *I AM: The Power of Discovering Who You Really Are*, I give a detailed explanation of how our self-concepts generate our thoughts, emotions, and actions, as well as a description of my process of awakening. Suffice it to say here, after perceiving that I was 100 percent in charge of my life, there was nothing left to shield me from the implications of this truth. I could never crawl back under the rock of ignorance again and blame the world for my problems. The sole creator of my experience was revealed: I AM.

For me all it took was one instant of reflection. While in a seminar on the psychological nature of buying and selling in the stock market, information I was presented with set off a chain reaction inside my mind. Many of my long-held beliefs on the nature of life fell like a string of dominos. Simultaneously a whole new way of looking at life was revealed that brought me answers to my deepest questions. That's all I needed to come face-to-face with the person responsible for how I had been going through life and for how my life seems to be going right now. If I don't like what I am creating in my world, I—and only I—have the power to change it. No one can think for me, perceive for me, feel for me, or act and react for me. In this eternal moment, I am my own creator.

You never know what events will inspire you to act. My creative impulses were triggered when I least expected them to be. Although I graduated college with a degree in business, spent most of my adult life in the world of finance and had no experience as a writer, these facts were irrelevant when I decided to honor the insights I'd had by writing a book. As far as I was concerned, there were no limits. The core reason for all human action and reaction, joy and suffering had been revealed! I felt like I had found the Holy Grail, and I wanted to share the knowledge with every person on the planet. A creative geyser erupted within me that desperately needed an outlet. That's when I began to write.

It was as if the information needed to come out on to paper. Like a pregnant woman two weeks past her due date, I could no longer contain the material. I had no fears, as there was nothing except possibility and opportunity in front of me. It felt as if this massive awareness was oozing out of my pores. Either I was going to talk everybody in my social circles to death about my remarkable discovery, or I was going to publish it and let everyone interested in the information find the way to it on their own.

The moment I made the decision to write, words began to flow. The stream of ideas and words didn't stop for over a year. Every night I made my way to the public library, where I would sit at a desk and write for anywhere from three to six hours. At the beginning I had no outline, no title, and no idea what was going to come out of me each night when I sat down. But this didn't scare me. It only added to the excitement.

I had one ritual. Before I started to write each night, I said, "May I connect to bring forth what the majority of people want to understand as it relates to living a peaceful and fulfilling life." After this, I just let it flow for hours on end.

It's important to understand that a creative impulse can take on an expanded life that's much bigger and has many more dimensions than your initial plans recognized. My creative mission did not stop with the manuscript. I also established a private consulting practice called Truth Serum and designed a website (**www.truthserum.net**) to spread the word about my understanding of the nature of life. As each new step was taken, I had to step willingly into a new version of myself. As Howie 2.0 was being formed, I had no idea how people would react. The beautiful and liberating thing was, I didn't care! I was following my heart's desire. I was honoring my inner voice and my life's purpose.

Are you are wondering how I know that it is my life's purpose? The answer is simply the peace and state of full contentment I feel each time I act in accordance with it. When I am speaking or writing about the information in my book and on my website, I feel in perfect harmony with the universe. That's how you will know your purpose, too.

There isn't a single person alive who does not have something to offer to the world. Each of us is a messenger for the others. Your accumulated knowledge, based on what you have experienced through your journey thus far in life, is priceless wisdom. People need you to share your experience! Whether you are a cook, seamstress, sports star, parent, mechanic, divorcee, doctor, criminal, military person, runaway, accountant, recovered drug addict, editor, counselor, salesperson, small business owner, landscaper, manager, financier, guard, lawyer, executive, teacher, or student, or any number of other identities, you have a story to tell and a gift to give if you choose to share it.

Who you are is the foundation of your creativity. To try and be something you are not stifles and interrupts creativity. Later on your identity will be different and you'll have something else to give. Offer what you've got right now to the world. Create from what you know best. Allow yourself to be as you are and your creativity will flow.

At certain times, letting your message and creativity flow could seem hard to do. The truth is that it is neither hard nor easy, only related to the intensity of your desire to express yourself. You must be ready to be the version of yourself that presents particular information to the world ("I am a messenger for . . ."). You must be ready to be someone who is willing to step out from the shadows of life and onto the stage where you can be seen and your message can be heard. Your will and desire will carry you to the stage. But if you are unable to step forward yet, that simply shows you are not ready.

Often the mind tells us it is ready to move on, but the heart doesn't want to. Fear plays a big role in holding us back as our minds tend to fill the unknown future with projected images of worst-case scenarios. With an increase in your desire to become more creative or to build a new version of who you are, fear must be replaced by faith more optimistic future projections of personal possibility. Only you hold yourself back.

Creating Your Ideal Life? 137

At times personal growth can feel like you are standing on a busy street corner waiting to cross to the other side. On your side is everything you already know and do that has become stagnant and old. On the other side of the street a new experience waits for you, one that you will create based on everything you know in your heart of hearts that you have to offer the world and what this leads you to learn and do that is unfamiliar. As you close your eyes and imagine crossing the street and transforming your reality, you become filled with a fresh charge of excitement and joy. A new version of life is waiting to be realized that redefines who you are in the most fulfilling way.

However, you open your eyes and there you stand—in the same place on the same old side of the street. You can't get yourself to move. And, to add insult to injury, while you stand there waiting for your big moment of courage, three other people step right off the curb without hesitation and make their way safely to the other side! You look at these people and wonder how they do it when you know damn well that what you have to offer is "just as good, if not better." Emotions such as anger, frustration, resentment, and sadness run through you as you stand frozen on the spot, feeling like you're wearing a pair of cement shoes.

So what does the ability to step forward and create anything new come down to? What causes some people to walk freely forward into the reality of their dreams and others to feel stuck and unable? Pure desire.

All action stems from desire. What you desire in life comes from what you feel you need in order to fulfill who you believe that you are ("I am *this*," "I am *that*"). You will stay stuck on one side of the unfulfilling side of the street until the belief becomes intolerable. At this point your desire will increase to a level that produces action. Then you will step off the curb and begin your journey to a new way of life, a life more aligned with your dreams.

The main reason many people never allow their creativity to flow is that they are willing to tolerate frustration. It does not have to be this way for you. You can decide, right now and right here, in this instant, to move forward and unleash your creativity. You have a blank canvas in front of you. This moment, like every other moment in your life, is a moment of free choice. A whole new life of experiences awaits you. Whenever you have a creative dream, or any idea at all in your head, you will be faced with the same question, "How badly do I want to make my dream become real?"

There are no limits in life except the ones you set for yourself. When you finally decide you want to accomplish something badly enough, you will be willing to try and fail and then try again. The secret that separates those who succeed from those who stop easily is the ability to learn what is needed from the experience of failure and then move on. Where failure is the stopping point for those who never go on, for the successful creative person it is feedback from a supportive universe: information they need to get to their ultimate destination. Who you are is not defined by your experiences, but rather by how you respond to them! If you remove negative connotations associated with failure from your mind, you will be free to take risks, and your creativity will explode.

True creativity is not forced; it flows effortlessly from an open mind that does not seek the approval of others. And what comes out of such a mind is directed, shaped, honed into a form that aligns perfectly with a person's intent. Self-expression knows no boundaries. Through unfettering your mind, you allow yourself to bring forth something new.

A big part of my counseling work at Truth Serum is offering self-reflection to others in a way that expands their own understanding of who they are and of what they are capable of creating for themselves in life. This is the start of the path to open up creative possibility. This process always begins with a self-reflective question such as, "Who am I?" By asking, you are demonstrating the desire to know. This opens a space in your mind that the self-fulfilling universe will immediately respond to with potential answers.

As the answers immediately show up in the people, places, and events of your life, your ability and willingness to connect them to your questions will be based on how ready you are to accept them. By accepting the answers that will allow you to take more creative control of your life and the energy of your personal expression, you will be changing who you are. By accepting these answers and the implications they have on your life, you are demonstrating an even deeper level of desire for personal change and new possibility. No moment is wasted in bringing you the answers, including this one right now.

You have the power to choose your destiny. Your creativity is only limited by your belief in you. When you open to receive the answers to your questions, you begin to see how you are choosing the speed at which you manifest your desires. You are in control of who you choose to be and what steps you decide to take in life. No matter what the area of creativity, your desire of intent to develop it will determine if it takes a month, a year, or a lifetime.

Desires that aren't acted on will remain only as fantasies. The final step in any new expression is in the creative act. You must cultivate the willingness to act on the new choice you have made for yourself and your life. This is what sets the conditions for your dreams and desires to become real and experiential. When you begin to act in accordance with your deepest desires, you are demonstrating what you truly believe as possible regardless of the results. It is the same thing when you don't act. The only thing the universe can respond to is whatever you demonstrate you truly believe in. Have faith in your creative power and its ability to lead you to a life of conscious creativity.

Throughout this creative process there will be perennial ups and downs. Accepting each for what it is offering you will be a key to your continued ability to accept the challenges along the way, learn from them, and keep going. *You are limited only by the depth of your desires.* With consistent desire and strong intent, any one of your creative dreams can be realized. The entire obligation to make it happen is up to you. No one can write the story of your life for you, because on some level you have to agree to it. The reality is that you are always in charge.

As my personal journey of self-expression continues, my daily intent is to continue to act in accordance with the faith that I feel in my heart rather than the fear that resides in my head, to listen to the inner voice of truth that guides me with complete accuracy, and to continue to expand into more creative possibility, serving others in the process.

The following quotation sums up my desire for myself in my lifetime, and I offer it to you now as inspiration for your own creative journey. These words were written on a church wall in Upwaltham, England: "I will not wish thee riches, nor the glow of greatness, but that wherever thou go some weary heart shall gladden at thy smile, or shadowed life know sunshine for a while. And so thy path shall be a track of light, like angels' footsteps in the night." My deep thanks to who you already are in this moment and for everything you have overcome to get here. May you always experience the best in your creative choices.

Building a Better Generation

Rebecca Linder Hintze

The hope of our future depends upon our youth. If you're a parent, grandparent, or teacher and sometimes feel as if you have no influence, remember this quote by William Ross Wallace: "The hand that rocks the cradle is the hand that rules the world."

Recently, I had a terrific experience with one of my daughters. On her own, she volunteered to provide service to a family in need. After completing her commitments to this struggling family, she shared her experience of serving. I felt emotional listening to her describe her response to the events surrounding this opportunity. While watching her eyes and expressions, and listening to her tender thoughts and feelings, I noticed how much more advanced and wise my daughter seemed to be than I was at the same age.

I shared the listening experience with my mother (who I knew would be a proud grandmother). My mother was thrilled, and she said to me, "That's perfect! Your job is to turn out a better generation." My mother pointed out that many times parents feel competitive with their children. But really, parents should be ecstatic to watch their children outdo them. She said, "If every generation put out a better generation, our world would be a better place. What better tribute to a family heritage than to send out a more improved version every few decades?"

How can we influence and improve a generation of youth? Here are ten suggestions for parents and grandparents, teachers, and even loving, influential friends:

1. ***Trust them.*** Children are born with inner knowing and are often more in tune with what's right and best than their parents realize. Often, adults shut this inner knowing down in their offspring by projecting fear and judgment, and by pressing rules of social conditioning upon them. Usually, our youth will naturally gravitate toward greatness if we trust them and allow them to be

authentic, remove our judgments and fears, and let their intuitive nature thrive and guide them.
2. **See them.** Parents and teachers frequently project their personal issues onto youth. What a parent fears will often play out in the life of a child. This can cause youths to act out in ways that are not natural to them. Consequently, destructive family patterns pass on, even when the behavior isn't instinctive to a child. When parents see their kids—who they really are—the youth are more apt to show up great. (For more on healing destructive patterns, see my book *Healing Your Family History* (Hay House), where I describe solutions in greater detail.)
3. **Listen to them.** When parents and teachers are self-absorbed, they rarely listen to young people. Listening is more than hearing what is being said. It is recognizing all that's being communicated, and that includes paying attention to non-verbal cues. Doing this effectively requires a parent to step outside his or her own perception and see another's point of view. Children who are heard are more apt to keep the communication lines open—a critical factor in establishing and maintaining a healthy relationship.
4. **Validate them.** Once children are heard, if they are validated, they feel more confident and empowered to succeed. Validation is the key to overcoming any relationship block. When we feel validated, we feel loved and supported. This process is absolutely essential to supporting healthy growth and self-esteem.

5. ***Encourage them.*** Today, most of the information communicated in our world is negative or critical. As a society, we seem to miss this essential point—encouragement does far more good than any form of criticism, judgment, or negative influence.
6. ***Support them.*** Many youth today feel unsupported—either the adults in their world don't do enough to sustain them or they do too much and consequently hinder their potential. Real support comes when the right balance is maintained. Know what your child can handle and still be successful. Then, maintain that balance.
7. ***Protect them.*** Healthy boundaries are essential throughout life. Teach youth to stay away from destructive influences that will literally ruin them—and stop them if they head down a destructive path. Adults don't let two-year-olds play in a busy road for good reason! There are many dangerous influences that threaten the lives of youth and keeping kids away from them is just as important as removing a baby from a busy road.
8. ***Guide them.*** Although teenagers think they know it all, good advice is best found from a loving, wise, and caring adult. I remind my teenage clients frequently that their friends may seem smart, but really they don't know too much. Share your experiences and learning with youth and teach them correct principles that will foster long-term success.
9. ***Accept them.*** Remember in first grade when you colored a picture and you thought it looked great? If you saw it now, would it be a Rembrandt?

Probably not. Young people will often do their best and still it won't be as perfect as you can do now. What's not perfect is really perfect! We learn by making mistakes and healthy youth make a bunch of them. When I see a toddler throwing a fit, I smile and say, "He's perfect at being two." It really is okay when a teenager acts like a teenager and a wiggly boy acts rambunctious.
10. **Love them.** Living all these tips in relationships sends a loud message—that you love your child or young friend. Ultimately, that's all you can do to support anyone—and it's the best thing you can do. Truly, all things will fail but love!

Your secret to being successful at accomplishing this list lies in your ability to apply these same solutions to yourself. If you find it a struggle to live a life based on these philosophies, you'll naturally resist applying them in relationships outside you.

If you are a person who trusts your judgment, sees your value, listens to your inner knowing, validates your feelings, encourages and supports yourself in healthy ways, has healthy boundaries and protects your environment, receives helpful guidance in a loving way, accepts your weaknesses and strengths, and has self-love—you'll find that guiding a better generation to emerge will come naturally.

As you heal, apply these principles—first, within. Next, use these tips in your relationships with family members, or with those you love and guide.

Creative Decision-making

John Darrouzet

Throughout my years of work as an attorney, software engineer, and professional writer, I have observed that clients have the greatest difficulty with the single most important thing leaders are supposed to do: make creative decisions.

Usually what they engage themselves in are unexamined processes—false, sometimes bad, and usually ugly processes. In general I find their responses insufficient. They make choices as if they are in some sort of gambling casino, or make judgments as if their brains are plugged into a computer's infallible algorithm. In effect, they are using choices and judgments as surrogates for the real thing. To avoid both rash decisions and indecisiveness, they are failing to see that what they lack is a common sense approach to a process that could regularly result in creative decisions. But what is that?

When a "leader" makes a choice among alternatives prepared by others, the "leader" is at the mercy of the "followers" who are making the proposals. When a "leader" makes a judgment based on evidence and reasons of the past, "the leader" is backing into the future with enormous vulnerability to blind spots. The "leader" is really following.

Ultimately, I came to realize that the heart of true leadership is making creative decisions. But since not all "leaders" are creative, on behalf of my clients (and myself, for that matter) several years ago I felt compelled to take a journey to try to answer the following question.

Issue: Do you want to adopt a more creative way to decide issues?

If you initially have a mixed response (a "yes" and "no" at the same time) to the posed question, don't worry. Not all questions are issues. Issues try to expose a specific dilemma you face, often an apparent contradiction or at least a paradox. Being initially double-minded is a telltale sign of the problem of decision-making itself. What I was looking for, and think I have found, is a single-minded approach.

My journey began when the baseball movie *Bull Durham* first came out. My lawyer friend, Bob Provan, and I went to see it in Kansas City while we were at a boring law conference. Afterwards, Bob introduced me to Christopher Vogler's way of analyzing movies. In his book, *The Writers Journey: Mythic Structure for Writers*, Vogler uses his interpretation of the hero's journey to show writers how stories are structured. Given Bob's natural storytelling ability, he easily dissected the movie we had just seen, right in front of me.

But as he described the hero's journey, I had one of those "Aha!" moments. I realized that its stages were analogous to the internal process I had experienced when helping my clients make creative decisions.

To demonstrate how Vogler's approach to heroic structure works, I want you to pick your favorite American movie. Right now. While you're thinking about your movie, I'll tell you my version of Vogler's structure of how your movie flows.

Got your movie in mind? (Be sure to pause at the end of each numbered item to capture a scene in your mind. Words in quotations are meant to indicate metaphorical concepts, not literal ones.)

Okay, here we go:

1. In the beginning of your movie, you see your hero in his or her "ordinary world."
2. Next, your hero is called to an "adventure."
3. But your hero is reluctant.
4. Then your hero encounters a wise one who encourages the hero to go forward.
5. So your hero passes through a first threshold, leaving the "ordinary world" behind.
6. Your hero meets "tests and helpers."
7. Your hero reaches an "inner sanctum" where the hero faces personal questions.
8. Your hero endures "the supreme ordeal."
9. Your hero seizes "the sword."
10. Your hero takes "the road back."
11. Your hero experiences a "death and a resurrection."
12. Your hero returns to his or her "ordinary world" with the "elixir."

I hope this worked suggestively, if not perfectly, for you. On my blog (**http://special counselfordecisionmakers.blogspot.com**) you can read a blow-by-blow illustration of this journey using the movie *High Noon*.

Do you recognize how the Hero's Journey, as a mythic structure, may be thought of as having universal application to fiction? Most current American movies employ such a structure.

Of course, early on I realized that I would have to modify it for the purpose of decision-making. First, to educate leaders about this model without requiring their agreement in advance, I knew my model would have to incorporate questions that pointed to the milestones of the process along the way. Second, to learn which questions best paralleled the journey of the hero on an internal basis would require me to go on some journeys myself, both fictional and real-life ones.

Over years of study and testing on real clients, I undertook that task and transformed the 12 stages of the hero's *external* journey into 12 milestones for the decision-maker's *internal* process.

Decision-Maker's Path™
1. Where are you coming from?
2. Where do you want to go with the issue?
3. What are you waiting for?
4. What are your wise ones generally advising?
5. How are the pros and cons of your issue balancing out?
6. What are the "Powers That Be" saying?
7. What is your real agenda?
8. What facts and reasons are you contending with?
9. What insights and oversights are emerging?
10. How are you going to tell your decision?
11. What are you willing to risk to gain what you can only hope for with your answer?
12. What is signaling you that the decision you discern is the right one?

The moment of creativity in the process comes at milestone 9 on the Decision-Maker's Path™, a moment that is parallel to item 9 in the Hero's Journey when the hero seizes the sword. If you're interested in having more information about this, on my blog (**http://specialcounselfordecisionmakers.blogspot.com**) I illustrate the Decision-Maker's Path™ in my summary of the movie *It's a Wonderful Life*. I also present a combined analysis of Hero's Journey and the Decision-Maker's Path™ in my retelling of the movie *Witness*.

In each of these retellings, there is no creativity if the hero does not seize the sword. Likewise for the Decision-Maker's Path, it is when the decision-maker sees the emerging insights and oversights that creativity comes into play. When the decision-maker apprehends the insight and appreciates the oversight, the person makes something of them.

But what is being made?

Generally speaking, the person deciding is giving his or her free assent to take a specific future course of action that is presented symbolically in what is apprehended and that answers the issue in question.

Specifically speaking, it comes in *High Noon* when Will Kane apprehends the insight that he will most likely be fighting the bad guys by himself. It comes in *It's a Wonderful Life* when George Bailey feels strange and apprehends the insight that shines light on his appreciation of the near oversight in shaking Potter's hand. It comes in *Witness* when Rachel unashamedly reveals her beautiful self to John Book and he lowers his head, realizing he must not fulfill his desire for her as long as neither knows how to bridge their two worlds.

It is when the decision-maker gives his or her assent that he or she becomes valuable, accomplishes the central task of the path's mission, fulfills the significant purpose, and incarnates the vision presented. It is at this moment that the person becomes a creative decision-maker. And when that happens, the creative decision-maker becomes the *de facto* leader.

To see how this plays out in other movies, I work with clients now in customized retreats, selecting from numerous movies ones that depict the various stages and steps. For example, with *Witness* you have the opportunity to feel the tension between the spiritual and material worlds in the midst of a love affair that tries to bridge the gap but does not succeed. With *The Collector*, you have the opportunity to remind yourself that some take the wrong approach to conquering the gap by domination or submission. These two movies help deal with the split in the world where we are coming from.

With *Lawrence of Arabia* you see how one person can make a difference in the world as he struggles to learn where he really wants to go. By contrast, with *The Strange Case of Dr. Jekyll and Mr. Hyde* you are warned what not to want: to conquer nature.

When you are hit with inevitable reluctance to change, you want to learn what's holding you back. With *Casablanca* it's Rick's problem of dealing with his hurt at the hands of a woman. In *Hamlet* it's a matter of timing. What are you are waiting for?

With *Bull Durham* you see the desirability of finding wise counsel. There are coaches and players and wise women to boot. But with *The Godfather* you see that tribal advice is not always the best. With *The Magic Flute* you experience the philosophical young prince seeking to save the princess in a not-so-ideal world. From whom? Why?

When you are ready to move from the general to the specific, from concept to reality about your issue, typically you face an identity crisis. With *Bourne Identity* and *Manhunter* you face this problem for different reasons. You have lost your identity and must fight back to step through the door of the first threshold. You see what the pros and cons of your issue are and especially how they affect you personally.

Next you face the existential problem by confronting what the "Powers That Be" say. With *A Man for All Seasons* you get to know the discipline is takes to face a tyrant. With the *Rules of the Game*, you understand the powerful conventions of society. With *Kiss of the Spider Woman* you see the power of daydreams. Then, in stark contrast, you want to approach *The Gospel According to St. Matthew* where you see a political take on the story of Jesus.

Next you consider your personal agenda. With *Citizen Kane* you get to consider money. With *Who's Afraid of Virginia Woolf?* you deal with power. With *Body Heat*, sex. With *The Exorcist* you have the opportunity to deal with self-deception.

With *12 Angry Men* you have the opportunity to deal with fallacies and counterfeit arguments that undermine your ability to contend with facts and reasons about your issue. With *The Decalogue* you get to consider whether morality enters into the reasoning process. With *Seven* you see what happens when morality doesn't enter the process. Then with *The Passion of the Christ* you may want to consider the supreme ordeal endured at one sacrifice that changed the world.

To better understand how insights and oversights emerge from such ordeals, you may next consider three movies. With *The Lives of Others* you will see a conversion for the better due to an insight. With *House of Games* you will see a conversion for the worse due to an oversight. With *Field of Dreams* you will have the opportunity to see how the apprehension of insights works to build support for the decision you are making.

Next you may consider critical aspects of how you are telling the story of your decision. With *Cyrano de Bergerac* you may learn about the importance of telling it in your own words. With *Children of a Lesser God* you may learn about the significance of using your own sign language. With *The Last Temptation of Christ* you may learn the advantages and disadvantages of using your imagination. And with *Jesus of Nazareth* you may see how the story of a decision is more telling when it fits within the context of a life.

Once you are ready to tell the story of your own decision, you will face the toughest objections to it. What are you willing to risk to gain what you can only hope for by telling your decision? With *In the Line of Fire* you may see the lengths to which you must be willing to go to protect the truth of your decision.

With *The Departed* you will see what happens when the question of truth has long since been trampled under. With *Downfall* you will see the utter destructiveness that may possess those who try to live without hope. But with *Schindler's List* you will see the triumph of those who hang on to hope regardless of the odds.

Towards the end of the decision-making process, you will have the opportunity to consider four heroic endings to you journey's path. In each you may celebrate the decision of four different hero types and the receptions given it by the community: with *Paint Your Wagon* the wandering hero (value); with *The Shawshank Redemption* the warrior hero (mission); with *Romero* the martyr hero (purpose); and with *Doctor Zhivago* the visionary hero (vision).

Moreover, you may deal with four types of answers to issues: the magician's answer of *The Lord of the Rings*, the statesman's answer of *Chariots of Fire*, the sage's answer of *Cinderella Man*, and the saint's answer of *The Gospel of John*. In each you will see the importance of humility and significance of love in the decision-making process.

Nowhere in the curricula of my era of education was such an approach to decision-making taught. So I had to go way back to basics to find the earliest versions of the "method" I was discovering about creative decision-making. Since I nearly went mad in my search, what I found nearly blew me away.

In *Divine Madness: Plato's Case Against Secular Humanism*, Joseph Pieper discusses four ways in which Plato observed people "being beside oneself": 1) prophecy, 2) catharsis, 3) poesy, and 4) eros.

When I combined Pieper's analysis with Bernard Lonergan's *Insight: A Study of Human Understanding*, I came to realize that these four "mania" were actually four dimensions of insights received by human beings throughout the ages when they were in the throes of a decision-making process.

Thus, in today's business world, I now see "poesy" to mean creating value. Similarly, "eros" means being possessed by a significant mission. "Catharsis" means processes being healed on and by purpose. And "prophecy" means having a vision of where the creative decision-making leader wants us to follow. I began to see their impact on the exercise of our most defining freedom we have as human beings: making decisions. I came to see how the transformed Hero's Journey of the Decision-Maker's Path™ provided a series of repeatable processing questions, using the four perspectives of value, mission, purpose, and vision to fit the decision-maker's preferred leadership style.

Thus the proposed Decision-Maker's Path™ brings the best *value* to the task. While it is usually observed that people in leadership positions keep their methods of decision-making to themselves based on the concept that knowledge is power, if the Internet has demonstrated anything, it is that shared knowledge is more powerful and that transparent methods encourage better decision-making on behalf of the community.

The decision-maker who works within the suggested structure learns the best practices for the *mission* by repeated passes through the process. While there are few hard and fast rules for creative decision-making, those available are learned more rapidly and honed with more strength than otherwise via this approach.

The proposed Decision-Maker's Path™ is more attractive to people who want to make changes because its *purpose* is supported by the storytelling process of the Hero's Journey. The decision-maker's character will be recognized in the context of a story told about real life and work.

Finally, the creativity of this approach to decision-making is *visionary* because it allows its user to bring new light to issues in question each time the process is used. The decision-maker assents to the insight that emerges and sees any oversight in the light of the insight. Because there are as many perspectives as there are people concerned about an issue, the task of the decision-maker, once the insight emerges, is to take the lead, focus the followers on the insight so that they become one behind the course taken.

So now it is your turn. I invite you to take a Hero's Journey in your creative decision-making process around every issue of importance in your life.

Manifesting a Healthy Life

Kathi Handt and Jay Handt, DC

Chiropractic care is not about your back . . . it's about the quality of your life.

Manifesting a Healthy Life 157

For just a moment, pause and imagine what your ultimate healthy lifestyle could be? Remember, we're talking about the very best health and vitality, the optimum physical, mental, and emotional condition you would like to attain. If you're like most people, probably you have some trouble forming this image. That is the primary reason most people never create the quality of life they desire. Or you may be someone who has a very clear image of what you want, but the exactness of this image is restricted to one area of your life—for most people an area that has to do with wealth and the accumulation of material objects.

What you may not realize yet is that having whatever you want in life starts with the quality of your physical and mental health. Having control over those two aspects of your life will allow you to go after, and achieve, anything you want.

You can see how difficult it would be to achieve any goals if you were constantly suffering from poor health. How far do you think your creative process will take you if your mind and thought processes always come from a point of negativity, depression, and disease? If you've ever had an injury or illness, you can appreciate how important the quality of your physical and mental health is to creating and leading the life that you want to experience and enjoy.

In *First Things First,* organizational consultant Stephen Covey talks about doing what is important before doing what is urgent. The reason most people avoid doing the important things first is that usually they are some of the most boring, time-consuming, mundane chores. But these are the things that create the foundation for your dreams to be built upon. It's in painstaking preparation that peak performance and ultimate achievements are created. This principle is as true for your health and physical performance as it is for your career.

Has your curiosity ever got the best of you as you walked past a construction site, where you peeked through one of those cutout holes in the plywood wall? To your surprise, all you saw was a big hole in the ground on the other side. Perhaps months went by before you passed that way again, and when you looked again, it seemed as if nothing had changed. The same big hole was there and there was still no building. Did you begin to wonder what was going on? What construction crews are doing in this phase of construction is digging a very deep hole to create a stable foundation. And did you know that the deeper they dig, the stronger the foundation will be? Speak to any architect. Do you know what the hardest part of construction is? It's digging out for the foundation and putting in all the cement and footings.

Now, you can get away without doing all that. You can just build on a flat slab. Most homes in Florida are built like that. But what happens when a tornado comes through? That's right. You're left with a slab. You have no place to hide. My family found ourselves in close proximity to a tornado in Georgia one year, and what did they tell us to do? They told us to go into the basement. What's the basement? It's the foundation. It's the strongest part of the building. The building might blow away, but the foundation would still be there to protect us.

Preparation is the key to excellence. The Olympic downhill ski racer spends endless months and years training and fine-tuning skills, and training some more and fine-tuning some more, all in the hopes of coming in first in a performance that lasts not much more than 60 seconds. Of course, it's important to begin his training with the end in mind. Just imagine that he trains downhill for four years only to find out that he's scheduled to race cross-country.

Now let's assume for a moment that we all have the goal of a long and prosperous life. That's "the end in mind." So, what do you need to do first?

You need to make sure that your physical health and well-being is at an optimum level. The quality of your life is determined by how well your body functions. Your nervous system controls your body. What determines if your nervous system performs well is having an open and free-flowing connection between the brain and the nervous system. That "connection" allows messages to be transmitted and received by every cell in your body.

It would make sense, wouldn't it, that if there were a reduction of the flow of messages from the brain to the nervous system and then to the organs, tissues, and cells of the body, your health and well-being would be compromised?

We know that you understand where you want to go in your life, what you want to do, and how you want to do it. The most important thing you can do for yourself in addition to having an awesome vision of an end goal is to start with a nervous system free of interference. Chiropractic is a vital part of building your foundation for excellence and success because it is the only health care profession that focuses on the removal of the interference to the nervous system.

Of course, if that were the only thing we had to do, life would be easy. You'd drop your body off at the chiropractor for a couple of minutes and *poof* you'd have a perfectly functioning nervous system. But unless you take care of all the other factors necessary to create a healthy body and lifestyle, you're cheating yourself of establishing support. You have to build a healthy foundation.

You are probably wondering what else you can do to create a strong, stable foundation. There are five pillars that create a foundation for health and longevity. A nervous system free of interference is number one. Number two is your mental attitude. Research has shown that people who are negative, angry, bitter, nasty, or depressed tend to be physically ill more often than those who have a positive, outgoing, friendly, and flexible view on life. Thoughts create actions and so your thoughts play a major part in your health.

One of the best examples of the power of mental attitude is the placebo effect. Tests have been done with two groups. They gave the first group of patients sugar pills in lieu of an actual medication (without their knowledge). They gave a second group of patients the actual drug. Up to 70 percent of the people taking the placebo experienced the same, if not better, results than those who took the real drugs—and without the side effects of the drugs.

Unfortunately, some people experience the opposite effect. They take drugs, expect to feel side effects and, lo and behold, side effects appear. The placebo effect works equally well whether people are anticipating positive outcomes or negative outcomes.

Manifesting a Healthy Life 161

Anticipation and expectation play a huge role in the quality of your life and your health. You always get what you focus on, good or bad. So train your mind to focus on what you want rather than what you don't want. Fear is false expectations appearing real. If you expect something to happen long enough, it will come into your life. Good or bad health. It's your choice. Choose wisely.

The third pillar of good health is nutrition. The simple truth is that you are what you eat. As the adage goes: Garbage in, garbage out. Just look at the astronomical rate of obesity in this country and look at the typical American diet to appreciate this statement. We're not here to tell you that you have to be a vegetarian or give up foods that you love. Everything is okay to eat in moderation. But when you take the consumption of any type of food to the extreme, it can never be good for you. Whether it's a Big Mac and super-sized fries, or five pounds of carrots consumed every day, eating too much of a single kind of food will have a detrimental effect on your overall health. Good nutrition is based on balance, which is the best way to put diverse nutrients into your system.

Think about a high performance racecar that's polished, clean, and tuned up. Now, fill it up with economy-grade fuel. How well will it run? No matter how much you take care of the outside, if you put junk into it, it will never run well. How is this like your body? If you want your body to run like a finely-tuned race car, you want to make certain you feed it the best "fuel" to accomplish this, and that's the balanced mix of protein, carbohydrates, and fats. Each one is necessary for your body to function at a level of peak efficiency. Taking nutritional supplements might also enhance your vitality, but that's a topic for another discussion. You can eat what you want, just know that what you want will create not only the body that you have, but determines the upper level of health it is ultimately possible for you to achieve. I hope you are able to digest all of this.

Exercise is pillar number four. Very simply, if you don't use it, you lose it. Movement and flexibility are what life is about. Lack of movement and stagnation petrifies and paralyzes the body. Compare how much movement there is in a corpse to how much movement there is in a young child. Granted, death is an extreme example of stagnation, but in reality, the most vibrant super-seniors that we've seen are the ones who have had the most active physical lives. This doesn't mean you need to spend your entire life in a gym. Just think of exercise as any movement that you do on a regular basis: playing with your kids or grandkids, walking the dog, visiting a museum—any movement will contribute to keeping your body flexible. Every day, for at least one hour, you need to be doing something that engages the majority of muscles in your body. Remember, with exercise, it's about using it, not *abusing* it. Being a "weekend warrior" can often be just as detrimental as being a "couch potato." Balance is the key.

Rest is the fifth pillar. The purpose of rest is to repair, replace, and rejuvenate. When your body is at rest, it has the potential for cellular growth and cellular repair, as well as the ability to heal and revitalize. Every seven years, every single cell in your body has been replaced at least once. The only cells that are rarely, if ever, replaced are those of the nervous system (which is why it is so important to make sure that you're keeping your nervous system free from interference). Logic tells us that we would never grow old if we have a whole new body every seven years. Unfortunately, if you don't do something to maintain the quality and integrity of your current cells, when they are replaced, they are duplicated in the way the current cell exists. Healthy cells replace healthy cells. Weakened, compromised, sick cells reproduce weakened, compromised, and sick cells. That is why it is so important to incorporate the other four pillars into your lifestyle in order to create an optimally functioning body. Quality rest will fortify healthy cell production.

Rest is not just about getting a good night's sleep. Rest includes taking time off from your busy life to rejuvenate your mind and body. Rest means penciling yourself into your daily schedule for meditation, yoga, a power nap, or even for some enjoyable reading or listening to your favorite music. It's not about the hours of sleep; it's about the quality of your rest. It's essential that you learn how to turn off the outside world and get calm inside.

Four of the pillars we've just described are tangible. Proper rest, exercise, nutrition, and a good mental attitude are all things that each one of us can consciously choose to create. We can see our bodies and decide we need to exercise to get into shape. We know how much better a positive attitude feels. After a restful night's sleep, we feel refreshed and we notice that the dark circles under our eyes have disappeared.

We notice the difference in how we feel and look when we eat a balanced diet and get closer to our target weight (whether we need to gain or lose). But because we cannot see the effects of a nervous system that is compromised (until it is too late), it's not even in our consciousness to correct it. Yet, the cause of all illness and disease is a nervous system that, due to interference, is not functioning to its maximum potential.

Many people ask if they have to incorporate all five pillars in their lives. That is up to you. You can stand on three pillars, but the question is, for how long? You can deprive yourself of sleep, and you'll live. You can avoid exercise like the plague, and you'll live. You can screw up your diet, and you'll live. You can choose to pay no attention to your thoughts or even hold negative thoughts about everything, and you'll live. Without the full flow of information from your brain, through the spinal cord and out to all the cells in your body, you'll live. But your quality of life might not be what you expect, and you might not have the stamina to do all that you want to do or experience all you want to experience.

Actor Christopher Reeve had an accident. He broke his neck. He didn't break his back, his arms, or his legs. And he was paralyzed, not because his neck was broken, but because the spinal cord was severed, not allowing the flow of information to all those parts of the body below that point. Did he live? Yes he did. Did the quality of his life change? You bet. So I ask you: how important is it for you to take care of your nervous system?

When misalignments to the spine pinch nerves and slow the flow of energy, not all of the vital information that needs to be received by your heart, your stomach, your liver will be delivered, which in turn compromises your health and vitality. So how important is it to keep that nerve information flowing freely?

It's so easy to create the health and life of your dreams. Just incorporate the five pillars into your daily life and you'll make it happen.

The question we want to leave you with is this: Do you want just to survive or do you want to create a life that's worth living to the fullest? I asked my eldest patient, a woman who had just had her 97th birthday, what she would change if she could go back in time and change only one thing in her life. Her answer was, "If I knew I was going to live this long, I would have taken much better care of my body when I was 30."

There's no time like the present to create the future you've always dreamed of. Just take the first step and watch the magic take place.

Be and Grow Rich

Richard Aronow

A spiritual solution exists for every problem in our lives, including the challenge of creating wealth. I credit my own professional accomplishments in working through my company, Aronow Capital, with some of today's greatest business leaders, scientists, authors, and top minds to being an avid student of the laws of the universe and aligning myself with the forces of nature. These principles are responsible for everything I've created—and I am confident that they will work for every individual who applies them.

In a nutshell, the seven foundational steps to be and grow rich are:

1. Make a Decision to Be Wealthy. Being precedes the creation of wealth. If you want to be wealthy, you must decide to be wealthy. Your thoughts turn into real, tangible results in the world through the energy with which you infuse them and through the actions you take. This requires you to be aware of how you are being. Once you are aware, you can consciously choose to be an abundant, innovative, and energetically aligned person. This will give you the freedom to create anything that your heart desires, including the products, businesses, and relationships that are shown to lead to wealth.

Being wealthy always happens right now. Wealth doesn't come out of nowhere. It comes out of our present moment thoughts and actions. Envisioning an outcome in our minds and feeling the feelings that are associated with this outcome in our bodies are the two primary actions that manifest the outcome in the physical world. Before Microsoft reinvented the tools with which we do business and manage our lives, founder Bill Gates "saw" a computer on every desk. Similarly, before the 48-Hour Hollywood Diet generated $300 million in revenues, my partners and I "saw" millions of diet products being sold. Before building an airplane, the Wright Brothers "saw" people flying in winged machines. When you infuse your own activities each day with the spirit and energy of what you desire to create, your vision will soon take on a life of its own.

Deciding to be wealthy is a concrete vision that is manifested with persistent focus—if not today, then perhaps tomorrow . . . and if not tomorrow, then a year from now.

2. Pay Attention to What You Talk About. If you want to change your life, one very significant thing you can do for yourself is to change your inner and outer conversations. Negative conversations are expensive. They lead to poverty because they carry—and therefore manifest—the energy of lack, failure, and sickness. High-energy conversations (those energized by gratitude, excitement, love, healing, and beauty) make you feel good, nourish the soul, and ultimately lead to wealth. It's necessary to attend to your vision of what you want to create—not to pretend there are no obstacles, or deny their existence, but to embrace them as part of the process of manifestation of what you intend to create.

Your inner dialogue or self-talk reflects the fire of your soul. Your outer dialogue reflects your commitments and puts the inner energy into motion. Before you can enact a successful plan to create wealth and skyrocket your finances, you have to infuse yourself with spirit. Your soul needs to be on fire with enthusiasm. Then your actions will have more power than you can imagine for attracting the right people and resources to manifest your dreams and, ultimately, to create as much wealth as you could imagine.

3. **Join Your Spirit and Being with Infinite Consciousness.** Consciousness is a field of universal energy that you can access through your relationships. Your individual purpose is part of a larger process that includes everyone and everything in this field, so the most powerful thing you can do is to contemplate your part in this larger process. Then, when you join with one or more people who share the same spirit, desires, and goals as you, a field of powerful intelligence is activated around these relationships. Soon you discover that you have all the resources in your life that you need to succeed in your purpose.

All forms of wealth come from joining consciousness, energy, and spirit. Infinite consciousness has the power to create through multiple channels simultaneously in a way that no one person alone could traverse. This is why working harder is not a requirement of wealth creation. In fact, wealth comes from working with less effort rather than with more effort. It comes from maximizing your resources and connecting with a broader network of people and opportunities to do the same work in a shorter amount of time.

When you make a decision to be wealthy (and a part of this decision involves having what you want to the best of your ability), a collective consciousness is evoked that begins to work on your behalf. As William H. Murray wrote in his book *The Scottish Himalayan Expedition* (J.M. Dent & Sons, 1951):

"Until one is committed, there is hesitancy, the chance to draw back. Concerning all acts of initiative (and creation), there is one elementary truth, the ignorance of which kills countless ideas and splendid plans: That the moment one commits oneself, then providence moves too. All sorts of things occur to help one that would never have otherwise occurred. A whole stream of events issues from the decision, raising in one's favor all manner of unforeseen incidents and meetings and material assistance which no man could have dreamed would have come his way."

There's nothing that you really have to do in order to be wealthy. Spirit is in everyone, so when you tap into universal energy to create a business, product, or endeavor that many people value, the outcome is actually beyond your control. This principle is the same principle that made freedom the natural result of Thomas Jefferson writing the Declaration of Independence. His words were a decision that evoked a universal power that gave and still gives American citizens our freedom and inspire people around the world. This same power is available to you to create wealth in your life. It takes courage to make this decision, but it is the law of nature and getting out of our own way and being. When power-hungry people hurt each other with brutal economic force, it's like what an animal does when it kills another animal. Instead, learn to use higher consciousness to create.

Your heart is more powerful than your brain. However, your brain is ignited by the same energy that beats your heart. When you have awareness and connect the brain with your heart, you will be unstoppable. All people who are inspired—in spirit—are creating from a mutual desire, which makes the intention stronger.

Gandhi's work is the greatest example of drawing results from conscious intention. He ignited hundreds of millions of people in pursuit of one goal. No government, no punishment, nothing could sway them from the realization of their intention. The outcome of their mutual actions was to change the world.

Surrounding ourselves with other people by creating partnerships and mutual ventures is how the collective self creates wealth for individuals. Whenever we come together for a common purpose, collective consciousness begins to generate power, sort of like how an electric car generates power from six batteries. The energy of a central engine doesn't drive the car; it drives on an accumulation of energy. All genius, knowledge, and wealth come from the field of universal intelligence that has been organized by becoming in synch with other people's energy.

4. Ask Good Questions: The spirit of everything you do becomes a big part of you. We don't get what we want; we get who we are being. So live with passion, sing your song, and do your thing. Something that excites you also, surely, will be meaningful to others. More than once I have seen or experienced a creation take place in 48 hours that you might have imagined would take 20 years—just because the creator was creating from a spiritual focus. People and resources show up in answer to spirit, thus spirit-infused actions have an accelerated pace.

We carry our joy and potential around with us and we infuse it into our everyday lives. For this reason, instead of asking questions such as, "Why are people doing it this way?" that relate to thoughts of fear and

blame for what has happened in the past, we need to ask questions that lead us forward into new realms of experience. Such as:
- How will we be communicating in ten years?
- How will we be living?
- How will we create wealth?

Questions open the mind to receive answers, solutions, and information. Asking questions about the future creates possibilities. It taps us into our creative potential, and then we naturally come up with a plan.
- What might be?
- What could be?
- How can we?
- What could be but isn't?
- What could happen if we make a different decision?

We are living at the leading edge of a time in history when so much is possible. We have more power than before to do good or bad, so we must ask ourselves not, "Can we do *that* with the technology we have?" but "Do we have the desire to do it?" What are we doing with our abilities?

5. Narrow Your Efforts to a Specific Focus. To be wealthy and create more wealth you must have a purpose and a specific focus. Your focus shows up like footprints in what you do. Bill Gates' focus was on computers and software. The Wright Brothers' focus was on flight. Your love for what you are doing becomes a big part of who you are and infuses what you create with special spirit and your unique tracks on the ground.

Today we're all familiar with Kellogg's cereals. What many of us are less familiar with is the story of how The Kellogg Company got its start in 1906. Will Kellogg founded the company as the outgrowth of his work with his brother John making fiber-rich health food based on Seventh Day Adventist principles at a sanitarium and holistic healing center in Battlecreek, Michigan. They basically established a new industry by pursuing their vision of health for the masses.

If you're doing what you love and moving forward even if you are spending lots of time on it, your actions will feel effortless. Make a vision diary to keep track of your ideas and identify what you are specifically looking for. At this stage of wealth creation you are no longer contemplating the question: "Why isn't someone else taking care of this problem?" You are just doing what you are doing because you perceive a need and have chosen to respond to it.

6. Be in the Moment. What you do now—right now—is everything. There only, ever, is now. Ask yourself the following question if you don't know what to do next. "What am I choosing to do and who am I choosing to be to change the world for the better?" Write down the answers you receive. Higher consciousness is in communication with your spirit, whether or not you are talking. What are you doing now? What you are doing and being is talking for you.

In my own life, fear comes up when I think about whether or not I will be able to get where I want to go and when I feel as if I'm not able to see my way. But I know that fear is failure turned inside out. Its voice, which is the spirit of scarceness, creates failure if I indulge it. Furthermore, I've noticed that fear usually arises when I'm about to get what I want or move in a new direction.

If you want to create wealth you have to have the courage to stand up to the fear of poverty and move beyond it, which fortunately is not an issue when you're *being*. Fear is always in the future. There is no fear when you are in the moment—being. From this perspective you see there's possibility in every circumstance.

When you do what is in front of you to do, the right next course of action shows up, and then you will do that. Coming up with a plan and then enacting the plan is a good idea, at least to begin with, as long as you are open to letting the universe work for you in ways that you cannot imagine. The plan is only a starting place. You won't know why, but nature will bring the right people to you.

7. Let Go of Trying to Control the Outcome. Lose the desire to change and fix other people. As author Wayne Dyer says, it is none of your business. You can only ever change yourself and that change must begin inside you.

Be independent of your thoughts. Your thoughts are attempting to control the situation. But to create what we want in our lives we have to move beyond what we know and tap into the limitlessness of universal consciousness. What we know is limited, and it's usually wrong. At best it's a point of view. When we attempt to control outcomes we're only able to recreate what we already have.

Go beyond your thoughts by asking yourself, "Who am I?" and contemplating the idea that you are someone having thoughts. By watching the activity of your thoughts without "owning" them, you can become aware of the small voice within that is the real you. Like a radio that's receptive to many channels, you can tune your inner radio to the frequencies of your imagination and collective genius.

Be grateful for what is instead of comparing it favorably or unfavorably with what is not. When we are grateful we are in acceptance of what it. When we are grateful we are wealthy. If we're not grateful at the point of creating what we want, then we are poor indeed because the process of creation is our life. But if we're feeling grateful and good we are always wealthy with or without money in the bank. If we can feel grateful while we create, then making money is easy.

Opening your heart is essential to the creation of wealth. When your heart is empty, there is no room in your life for anyone. When your heart is full, there is room for everyone. The more room you have in your heart (which is the most powerful part of you), the more powerfully you can create anything you want to.

Wake up and don't concern yourself with yesterday or expend your energy on worrying about the future. Just keep moving forward on the plan you've created. Your heart energy creates wealth. So contemplate how to infuse everything you do with the spirit of gratitude, love, purpose, and success—and trust the outcome.

To summarize the seven principles of how every great fortune, wealth, and money in every category is created, I would say: Wealth is created through being connected with your life force, working together with others in a coordinated, unified way to achieve a common goal, and by tapping into universal intelligence. Always take action that is infused with desire, passion, purpose, and energy. Live in gratitude for what you have rather than regretting or bemoaning what you don't have. The feelings that come from this approach to life reinforce the high vibrational energy that attracts happiness, love, and prosperity.

Butterflies in Winter

Ann Moller

It was March 1, 2006. I was reading a book called *God Doesn't Have Bad Hair Days* by Pam Grout. My mom had given copies of this book to me, my sister, and a couple of our friends for Christmas that year. It's a book of experiments to test the existence of God, or whatever you want to call the higher power out there. The third or fourth experiment involves looking for butterflies over the course of your day. It has something to do with the principle that what you look for appears to you and what you intend comes true. Although it was deep, cold winter in Manhattan (an unlikely butterfly-spotting time and location), as I left my apartment in Hell's Kitchen I decided that I would do the experiment. Two or three other experiments from the book had worked well and I was having fun playing with a sense of magic in the world, in my daily life.

The backdrop of this story, by the way, is that I was under significant financial stress, so my desire for a sign from God, Goddess, both, whomever, was rather heightened. I was late on my rent and wasn't sure where the money would come from. The idea of a butterfly gracing my day as a signal that someone was out there looking out for me, and that magic just might truly exist, was highly compelling.

If I remember correctly, I took a trip that day to the Food Emporium on Eighth Avenue in the 40s, where they have a machine you can put your change into. It gives you a receipt, which you take to the customer service desk. They give you regular cash—as in paper bills—for it. Honestly, when you're down to your last few dollars and aren't quite sure how you're going to eat, it can be rather exciting to take a pile of change from the corner of your desk or the plastic bag where you've been keeping it, walk over to the supermarket in the cold, and dump your change into that metal tray. As you listen to it funnel down into the bottom, you can watch the green numbers on the black display box counting up the change, and while the last few coins clink and the rhythm of the change fountain slows down, you pray that the total will bump up to the next round dollar. It's satisfying to be able to say, "Ah! I had 36 dollars right there in change in my apartment! Aren't I resourceful to get it out and put it in that machine so I can actually use it to buy things I need?" Actually, I think once or twice my change even added up to 50 dollars or more.

Yes, this was one of those days: when a trip to the Food Emporium with a bag of change was a highlight and a triumph. Later that afternoon, I headed uptown to 72nd Street to drop off some timesheets at one of the temp agencies that I worked with. I usually liked to mail them to save myself trouble, but this time I really needed to get my paycheck that same week, so I went in person to ensure timely delivery.

It was very cold and gray outside. My eyes were peeled—on butterfly lookout. I was endeavoring to embody a kind of detachment from the outcome in combination with a positive, hopeful expectancy. Based on what I knew about the law of attraction, which the experiment was intended to teach me, it was important to be clear about your desire and to believe it would come true while at the same time to let it go on some level. In other words, I was attempting to play it cool, even though it was making me anxious that the day was almost over and I had yet to manifest a single butterfly sighting. I figured that someone or something was watching me and precisely monitoring the balance of faith, desire, attachment, and surrender that whirled around inside me. And if the balance was slightly off, no butterflies for me! Or worse, maybe all of this law of attraction stuff was a load of crap and I'd been investing my precious time and energy in a total fantasy. I scoured every visual plane I possibly could as I trudged (attempting to glide) down the block, and caught myself holding my breath several times.

Then something yellow and pink caught my eye in the window of a store to my left. I looked more closely, and saw a big, cheesy, plush toy butterfly, suspended there in the lower left quadrant of the display. It had black pinpoint eyes and a little smiley face. There was another one next to it, lavender-colored and smaller. They were hung on clear fishing line and floating there in the window. There was something delightful about how transparent the illusion was and also how much fun it was to imagine that they really were floating there. It was theatrical, actually, and I loved that. I stopped and took in the miracle—and smiled. I felt my heart burn with gratitude.

With that, I trotted merrily down the block to drop off my timesheet at the UPS store below my agency, where they have a mailbox, grateful for the sign that I was not alone, that my faith was not in vain, and that something bigger and smarter and braver than I was out there working with me to manifest my intentions. Of course I thought briefly that perhaps I had mastered the balance between the desire and the surrender. But isn't it funny that when the thing comes to you, you are so much more focused on gratitude to the world for delivering it to you than on what you may or may not have done to facilitate that delivery? At least for me, when something magical happens I am filled with a sense of wonder at the beauty of the world, of life, of all that is. My own role in the manifestation is important, but usually it seems less so than when I was actually going through the process. Instead, I often feel like, "Gosh, this was waiting for me the whole time! All I had to do was look!" Or perhaps surrender. Or receive.

When I got home, I had an email in my inbox from a friend that contained the word "butterfly" in the subject line. It included a beautiful story about a little girl and a butterfly. Another email that afternoon was about Wayne Dyer's book entitled *Inspiration: Your Ultimate Calling,* and the excerpt included in the email was a butterfly story, too. For the rest of the month, there was a flurry of butterfly stories, symbolism, and references in the online communications between the members of a class I was taking at Mama Gena's School of Womanly Arts.

That was a time in my life when I desired to break out of my cocoon. I felt stuck on many levels and I wanted a symbol of release, freedom, and faith. So among my close friends who call each other and ourselves "goddesses," I dubbed myself "the Butterfly Goddess." And I began to attract butterfly images everywhere I went.

I still do—sometimes in moments that feel just as desperate as that walk down 72nd Street in the depth of winter, and sometimes in moments when I am already feeling very strong and happy. Regardless, I am always grateful for the appearance of a butterfly in my life. It's a whisper to me: of my connection to all-that-is, of the deep wellspring of strength and faith that lies within me, and of the capacity for transformation, which is ever-present at my fingertips. After all, as a wise woman (my mother) once told me, "If you can find butterflies in New York City in the middle of the winter, you can do anything."

The Write Muse-IC

Laura Faeth

"The key question isn't 'What fosters creativity?' But it is 'Why in God's name isn't everyone creative? Where was the human potential lost? How was it crippled?' I think therefore a good question might be not why do people create? But why do people not create or innovate? We have got to abandon that sense of amazement in the face of creativity, as if it were a miracle if anybody created anything."
—Abraham Maslow

Albert Einstein, Socrates, Abraham Maslow, Frank Lloyd Wright, John Lennon. Now, there's a bevy of names synonymous with creativity. Each had vast potential, grand visions, or enormous talent. They're in a league of their own. As for me, I must have been daydreaming when God asked all of her newborn souls, "Who wants to be creative in their next lifetime?"

My soul probably has attention deficit disorder. I bet I was too busy staring at all of the angels' cool, flapping, luminous wings when God popped the question. Or perhaps the incredible sounds from an angelic choir kept me mesmerized. Whatever my excuse, for years it seemed as if God's magic wand (you know, the one that sprinkles the seeds of imagination and originality) had completely bypassed my soul.

As a teenager, my lack of creativity was blatant. A couple of guys in the neighborhood started a rock band with me, and I dreamed of playing to sell-out crowds in Madison Square Garden. We'd jam in my basement at ear-splitting decibels until the entire house shook. This made my mother, who feared for the safety of her delicate china dishes, *very* happy. It wouldn't have been so bad if any of us could actually *play* our instruments. No, when it came to performing music, the magic spark of talent certainly seemed absent from my DNA.

Although I could create hardly any melodic sounds with an electric instrument, it didn't take much talent to turn on the radio and *listen* to rock music. At age 15, a well-known rock band swept me off my feet. Their music and the sound of the lead singer's voice was my newfound mesmerizing angelic choir—except these guys didn't have wings or halos. They were pure rock 'n' roll.

The lead guitarist often quipped that they were just four great guys playing three great chords. He's full of baloney on rye. God's magic wand dumped an entire vat of creativity and talent on *their* souls. But because their musical gifts brought great joy into my world, I wasn't jealous.

Over the next two decades, I got married, had a couple of kids, and life seemed damned near perfect. The band's music was still integrated into the fabric of my life and continued to bring me a sense of completion. I had everything a woman could ask for.

Well, maybe not *everything*.

A feeling of restlessness arose within. A part of me felt unfulfilled. Then one day, out of the blue, my soul decided it was time to spiritually wake up, to remember my life's purpose—all because of that rock band I'd followed since adolescence.

Yes, the band and their music triggered a cataclysmic spiritual awakening that shook me to my foundations. I'd been wondering why I was so drawn to their music for two decades, when WHAM! A future vision encompassed me. In the flash of a digital camera, I went from, "Ho-hum, what's the meaning of my existence?" to knowing beyond a shadow of a doubt my life's mission: I would write a book. Not just any book. A book that would braid together two seemingly diametrically opposed subjects: spirituality and rock 'n' roll.

Spirituality *and* rock music? What a bizarre concept! And me, a writer? Hogwash. I'm not creative. I have no idea how to compose a manuscript. This was the most absurd, twisted vision a person could have. Nonetheless, the awakening unleashed a hidden aspect of myself I never knew existed and, in the following months and years, creativity and insights poured out of my head as if the Hoover Dam had burst.

The girl who could barely strum her guitar strings entered the magical realm of the artist. It was a fascinating, albeit unfamiliar and intimidating world. How does one tap into creativity and conjure interesting, unique perspectives? I wasn't sure.

The shockwaves from the awakening lingered, and a sense of purpose and trust permeated throughout my being. For this process to unfold, it was essential to trust that everything I needed was already within me. I just had to discover it. As a result of knowing my

"Mission Impossible" assignment (*Thou Shalt Write a Book about the Human Soul and Rock 'n' Roll*), I set aside time every day to allow my creativity and writing to bloom.

I wrote anything and everything that came to mind. At first, it was mostly *dreck*. But by not censoring my work, it created a safe place for my soul to blurt out whatever it needed to blurt. Long-forgotten memories of my childhood streamed forth. Silly, nonsensical concepts wanted expression, so they, too, were given a home. A humongous, cosmic kitchen sink of insights was recorded. The result wasn't elegant, and lots of it didn't even make sense. But it seemed that for the first time in my life, I allowed my psyche to run amuck, and—Oh, my heavens! —what a field day it had.

Yet I wondered: Where does the compulsion, the impetus to create, stem from?

For me, it was propelled by the desire for self-discovery. My soul wanted me to know my true spiritual identity and to share my insights through the written word. Like a seed that needs sunshine and water in order to grow into the magnificent tree it will one day become, my creativity needed to be nurtured and allowed to blossom. This realization eventually led to an understanding of the essence of creativity: inspiration.

The word inspiration means, "immediate influence of God or a god." The desire to comprehend my long-term attraction to a rock band, and the question of why their music touched my soul so profoundly, provided me with a source of inspiration. It was a catalyst for me to explore my spirituality in a unique and creative manner.

As I traveled down the Yellow Brick Rock 'n' Roll Road of Self-actualization, the band's music frequently spawned incredible insights and images . . . especially while zooming down the highway in my car. It got to the point that, whenever I started to drive, my mind was like a dog whose owner jiggles its leash. I'd get all excited and start foaming at the mouth as creative juices dribbled down my chin. Since driving and writing don't safely mix, a solution came via the digital tape recorder. Now I could blurt out the mother load of Aha's! that spewed forth at 70 mph and transcribe them safely later at home.

Some research suggests creative inspiration takes place when our brain generates a big burst of alpha brain waves, which generally occurs when we're in a relaxed state. Driving can induce a semi-hypnotic state of mind. Add the music and WHAMO! I had a powerful recipe for creativity at warp-speed ahead.

Over the years, fans of the band have commented how certain songs contain very unusual lyrics, almost like a secret message. While jotting down some spiritual insights one day, the tune "Gonna Raise Hell" nudged me. While I enjoyed the music, I'd never given the lyrics much thought. But my intuition kept bugging me to pay attention, so I finally went to a lyric website. Wow. In a burst of illumination, I'd cracked the code! Hell isn't just a place with a pitchfork-wielding dude. Hell, in metaphoric terms, is symbolic of our state of mind or a level of consciousness! "Gonna Raise Hell" in my twisted mind became,

"Gonna Raise Consciousness." We're spiritually waking-up!

Despite listening to some of the band's tunes for a quarter of a century, this revelation launched me on a musical beachcombing expedition into their lyrics, and I discovered boatloads of new twists that previously went right over my noggin. Since the lead guitarist was known for his double- and triple-entendres, searching for hidden meanings or themes in the band's lyrics was like going on a treasure hunt, and it gave me lots more to write about. Hearing several specific song lyrics in a new light provided additional insights regarding the healing power of music and supported my perspective that all of our souls are energetically connected.

During this phase, I noted that creativity begets creativity. Like rabbits, creativity multiplies exponentially. The more I wrote, the more the inspiration and insights flowed. I learned to type really quickly! The down side was that the exorbitant amount of awful writing was piling up. A single paragraph lasting 300 pages is not "writing." It's creativity with a hemorrhage. The wild, bucking stallion of my creative insights needed to be harnessed. My writing needed structure.

I knew that different kinds of music followed specific patterns. We don't mistake classical music for classic rock because a rock song has several structured parts, which, along with other elements like rhythm, tempo, and melody, make it distinctly and undeniably rock 'n' roll. This template provides a foundation to build a song. I needed a template to follow in order to give form to my writing. Yet I had no idea how to do that.

It was time to face the music and cross a line that all artists must traverse: show others what I'd written and ask for guidance. Even the best writers need an editor. The thought caused severe heart palpitations. *What if my writing totally sucks? What if my insights are stupid?*

If it hadn't been for my awakening, I'd never have had the nerve to show my work to anyone. But I trusted that somewhere deep within my ramblings lay diamonds of wisdom to be unearthed by objective parties. Other people: women in my writer's group, book loving friends, and whoever else I could find, gave me valuable feedback. Sure, sometimes their comments weren't sugarcoated and stung a bit. But, ya know what? I was right. There was a buried treasure of worthy and insightful nuggets hidden in my manuscript. Their suggestions provided direction and helped me organize my discursive thoughts. Now I had a clearer path to follow.

Over the course of six years, I edited and revised my book a gazillion times. I was proud of my creation. Then the manuscript came back from an established editor. My baby looked like Freddy Krueger had slashed it to pieces. Huge chunks were deleted. She thought the tone of the last third of the book felt very different from the rest of the manuscript and needed to be totally reworked. I bawled my eyes out for two days.

For years I'd agonized over every sentence, pruned and edited out half of what I'd written to help make my narrative tighter and thought I'd actually learned how to write in the process. Now I had to ask, "Was I a complete failure? Did I really have the talent to write a book on spirituality and rock music?"

A friend tried to cheer me up and told me creative folks sometimes refer to this phase as the "Dark Night of the Soul." Felt more like, "Black Hole of the Soul . . . Never to See Light Again." But all was not lost. The band came to my rescue. I read an interview by the guitarist that helped everything shift. He commented that sometimes he'd work on parts of a song for a decade or two before finishing it. Wow. A three-minute tune could take years to evolve. Hmm. Maybe that's a message for me.

Traveling down the road of self-discovery, we often hit a wall and come to a crossroads: Should we throw in the towel or call upon every molecule of faith and believe in ourselves? Seeing that my last name is pronounced "faith," I chose the latter.

Sometimes we need to grow and evolve before a song or a book can be "complete." Like the little seed that contains the genetic blueprint to mature into a giant oak, it appears any creative work has an energy or consciousness of its own. My manuscript was waiting for me to catch up to speed so that it could become a mighty oak among books.

This was just one more lesson in the life of anyone pursuing a creative endeavor: Don't take things personally, let go of all attachments to your words, be patient, and have faith!

With a newfound sense of enthusiasm, I rolled up my sleeves and went back to the manuscript. The editor was right. Certain areas still needed rewrites.

But overall, she really liked my voice and noted where I had gotten it *write*.

I went deeper into the process and saw connections I'd missed; the crack in Hoover Dam sprung a major leak and more insights flowed. One revelation after another illuminated how the band helped me heal my soul. Putting all that into words was the hardest work I'd ever done as a writer. Yet, in another way, it was the most rewarding. My appreciation for the soul connection between myself, the band, and their fans had never been stronger.

I wept at this realization. My life truly *is* blessed. This journey has given me an opportunity to discover my latent talents, a sense of self-worth, and provided a peek at my glorious potential. God's magic wand of creativity hadn't missed my soul after all. I had allowed fear and self-doubt to hide my brilliance. Deep within my heart, I now know that not only the gifted Albert Einstein's or rock stars of society can offer the world their creative boons. Every person has something unique to share.

It really is ironic. The girl who believed she was defective and lacked creativity discovered inspiration and the meaning of her life thanks to four great guys who play three great chords.

Power, Freedom, and Grace

Mary Jane Mahan

Creativity constantly wafts in the air around us like the sweet perfume of a rose bush. At any time we could jump up and snag a big, juicy blossom of creativity off the astral plane, inhale its fragrance with satisfaction, and then exhale aromatically via the pen onto the paper. The eternal question is why don't we? Instead of completed ideas and projects, why do we allow a disappointing cycle of creative pregnancy to continue that ends with our delicate thoughts dying in the bud? How could we encourage more blossoming, more thriving? To birth imagination into written words (or onto a canvas, or into a piece of clay, and so forth) takes a healthy umbilical cord and a devoted labor.

    I have learned several ways to trigger my creative juices and sustain them with enthusiasm until I produce blessed ink. Harvesting ideas into splendid, golden bales of written hay requires surmounting the ego's habitual downward pull to inaction. There are three inner fields, namely power, freedom, and grace, which I till regularly to open space for an access road that enables me to move actively towards creative inspiration. When the soil gets hard and stubborn, and the hay resists the blades of my thresher, I use these as tools to unearth ideas, a process that I call emotional leverage. Most importantly, I honor my mind as my master gardener. I engage in a daily practice of seeding self-love and weeding out self-destructive thoughts.

We are the stories we tell ourselves. Sages and spiritual masters have declared the most powerful words in language "I am." I can attest that "I am" is a state of beingness that is unlimited. If being were a Hollywood actor, it'd be a star of the highest order, a combination of Angelina Jolie and Brad Pitt. Being is simply the highest rung on the universal ladder. According to Neal Donald Walsch's *Conversations with God, Book 3*, life's natural order is be-do-have. Who we say we will be determines what we will do, and therefore what we will have. *Think and Grow Rich* by Napoleon Hill amply proved be-do-have as the common mindset of successful entrepreneurs, political leaders, and business tycoons. Simply put, if we wish to have unlimited results, we need to be unlimited and declare ourselves unlimited: "I am unlimited."

For many years, I lived like almost everyone else, caught up in a paradigm of have-do-be. "When I have enough money, then I'll hire an editor and write a book," I promised myself. My writing practice had the consistency of a half-baked cake until I started practicing better "I am Mary Jane" storytelling. "*I am power, I am freedom, I am grace,*" I now assert on a daily basis. More recently, I've elected to vividly link creative (be), writing (do), and process (have) respectively with the realms of power, freedom, and grace. I find an alchemical recipe for transcending writer's block, or more accurately, "self-concept block," so I can dance freely with the thoughts of my soul.

Creativity as Being

All creativity lies in knowing who you are. As I reflect on my school days, I sweetly recall feeling happy seated in a language arts, English, or communications class. Clearly I've always been a lover of language, yet my follow-through as a writer faltered. This was not for a lack of subjects, as endless shooting stars of brilliant creativity await my mind's lasso. However, to harness this cosmic bronco and ride the galaxy, first I had to believe that I could and deserved to be powerfully creative. Accessing personal power to fuel their inherent gifts is a courageous act of self-love evident in the work of writers like Marianne Williamson. Her passionate road map, *Return to Love,* illuminated a path of self-forgiveness for me that helped me start the brave process of dumping guilt about not writing and using my creative talents as much as I want to use them.

Thanks to personal development books and mystical teachings, I unlearned what an appropriate career path looks like and reemerged whole and perfect as I was created (thanks, Wayne Dyer). And from a powerful practice of "I am," I started writing again.

When I first started this practice, it felt like a farce and total lie. Reminding myself that it is our own light and not darkness that we fear, I slowly connected with the pain of my abandoned creative writing. I scarcely found the strength to journal, opting for other authors to hold the flashlight steady while I climbed out of my unworthiness cave. Once free from that low point, I began building my own "I am" platform on the basics.

"I am consistent, I am worthy, I am a leader." Like Darth Vader, I quietly sensed the presence of someone I hadn't seen in a long time: my inner straight-A English super star.

To ground this new foothold, I took a page from the playbook of other successful leaders and created a mental board of directors for guidance and support. I made my board president the embodiment of beingness herself: Mother Nature. In Nature, there is no struggle to grow, blow, or flow. The Tennessee River never doubts its power and the Sun doesn't force itself to shine. When I sit down to write and get a headache, I immediately know I am forcing thought instead of being my creativity. Because creativity is endlessly on tap, I return to the "I am" practice to open the faucet and be in the flow. How much water spills out is entirely up to me.

Writing as Doing

My philosophy is to always to take the biggest slice of the pie I can get, because there's an infinite amount of pie to go around. Love is infinite. If love were money, love would be a resplendent giga-zillionaire with whom I would align to write in freedom.

I am no different from anyone else in that I don't like *having to* do something. Feeling like I *have to* write is a yucky, difficult space, a place of do-have-be instead of be-do-have. It makes my office chair appear to me like a lifeguard stand in a prison with no escape from the blaring sun. Needlessly I fry myself with long, frustrating sessions of dribbling, fragmented sentences. Until I realign myself with "I am love," I cannot enter the cool water of the ocean and the ease of writing aligned with the flow of the ocean's current remains elusive to me. Therefore, I do everything in my power to make writing a pleasure and fun, rather than a requirement or a chore.

Because of my intrinsic love of complexity and freedom, I adore writing while listening to jazz. I willingly let John Coltrane's saxophone carve a groove in my soul, like his 18-minute masterpiece "Ole." Jazz improvisation is perfect inspiration for a writer. Imagine a bunch of musicians thrown in a room together with only a chord and a vague melody. Someone takes the lead and the rest follow, laying down tracks over the main chord. In that free-floating pool, musicians either sink or swim. The ones who sink thrash and drown in all the freedom, criticizing their every note. The ones who swim laugh at their mistakes and cannonball with confidence a second, third, and tenth time. They do whatever it takes. The awkward tadpole swims until a jazz player is born. The awkward writer swims in words and ideas until navigating words is second nature.

Although my writing can slice the water effortlessly, it also can feel like a hard-hitting swan dive. Heck, I think I must be a cat with nine lives, as I've gone unconscious under the waves so many times while trying to write. Here's what I remind myself: We are all free to float in writer's paradise or in a hellacious state of procrastination. Like the determined jazz player, I push upward until I break the surface of writer's block. Rough or smooth strokes,

I keep swimming. This is all that matters. This is the doing of writing.

Emotional Leverage

It is a supreme act of creativity to invent one's own tools for self-growth and healing. At a point of desperation, I invented a process called "emotional leverage" to take a quantum leap from confused to consistent. This process helps me to use my emotions to gain a greater vantage point on my circumstances.

A few years ago I found myself on a dire financial and emotional precipice. I was nowhere near being a working writer. Instead, I was cutting my entrepreneurial teeth painfully as an online network marketer. After 16 months of mostly insignificant results, something had to give—and fast. The answer came in a mentor's favorite piece of advice: *"Play a game you know you can win."* What clicked was that my earliest childhood success was as a gifted championship runner. Boys were not my first love. I loved track and field, especially the 200-meter sprint. If I could complete set after set of practice squats in the dead of Philadelphia winter, maybe I could use athletic training again to remember how to focus. Maybe I could leverage that feeling to succeed in a new realm.

Intuitively, I went back to the gym. Armed with Bill Philips' incredibly detailed *Body for Life* curriculum, I climbed on the weight sets to play. When the first riff of Van Halen's song "Jump" came over the airwaves, I was instantly transported back to a high school domain of dedication and confidence. The challenge of constantly focusing on switching out weights, clocking my time, and recording my progress felt welcome and gratifying. As I charted my daily workout, I also witnessed the miracle of having a new, more consistent relationship with my daily business planner. Two months into my gym membership, I made two massive sales in a row.

The awesome feeling of making a profit paled in comparison to regaining my self-esteem. I ran with the victory and became a master game player, transferring rusty skill sets into trusty new tools for achieving goals. For example, when I realized I was vague in giving directions (an important ability in network marketing), I sharpened my tongue and picked up the pace via accessing my "inner-waitress." For ten years I had excelled in the restaurant industry where trading precise information felt as natural as breathing. I leveraged this ability to the requirements of network marketing.

Dabbling in the abilities related to my past successes became a form of alchemy. I found I could step into new tasks as if I'd been doing them for years. It works in the creative realm as much as in the business realm. Leveraging feeling good is a game I play every day in every way to get my job done as a writer and businesswoman. After all, my ego is a professional at freeze-tag. I still slip and fall, yet I always get up to the sound of my schoolgirl giggling, *Home base, I win!*

Process as Having

Enjoying my finished products is a fabulous payoff to writing. I love getting to have what writers have: clean white pages of words spun of mystical gold. Because I always write in the supportive company of my spirit guides, who serve as my ethereal cheerleaders, I view the process as a team effort. Many hands make light work in my artistic efforts. In this manner, I manage to let go of wanting to control the outcome. What pours out of the top of my head is a rushing river of oneness that I do not claim ownership of except for my authentic voice. I experience writing as channeling. I am a vessel for the energy to be expressed. I am not an inventor, I am a receiver.

The roughest writing sessions I experience are when I get in the way of what wants to come through me. For instance, as I prepared to receive what wanted to be in this essay, I made peace with its voice being highly personal. Then, five minutes after that great accord, I decided it needed to "sound like an essay" (cue up dramatic music). I spent five days trying to write in a voice supposedly more scholarly, more instructive, and more "New York Times" than my own. The page resembled an intravenous drip hooked up to an emergency room patient. Then, somehow, I woke up, laughed really hard for 30 minutes, and effortlessly wrote eight authentic paragraphs in three hours.

Whenever I remember to align with love, the writing process feels like channeling heaven compared to building The Great Wall of China brick by brick.

Knowing that my acts of brilliance are simply "downloads," like Mp3 audio files available on the Internet, as opposed to being heroic feats makes writing more enjoyable for me. The pain of years spent hitting the snooze button instead of writing in the journal is all too fresh. (Wait! Was that just this morning?) Yesteryear, my self-identity as a writer resembled Snufalufagus from *Sesame Street*. I had heard how great writing was; I just never saw a pen moving in my hand.

Today I live in alignment with the order of be-do-have, so I literally run to the computer. That's because I am grateful to have who I'm being: Mary Jane, the regular writer.

Being our greatness requires managing the ego, that little inner voice that just loves to comment on our every move. Dr. Brian Alman, the internationally renowned hypnotist, describes the ego as a professionally paid critic who holds back-row season tickets to the dance performance of our lives. If we accept the reality that this critic is never going away, the ego dance can become a waltz on stage instead of a dive into the mosh pit back near row 50. Enter in grace as the ultimate Ginger Rogers.

Often I find myself so caught up in the process of writing that I forget to breathe and enjoy. For when my self-saboteur smells fresh meat, I invite grace onto the page to serve as my heroine. Elegant and merciful, grace knows no obstacles and she does not care what I look like. Grace allows me to throw the notion of process right out the window and opt for cruise control in the magical manifestation lane. Asking for it is surrendering to the unseen, waving the white flag when I've gotten terribly lost three pages in and I want to cry. My creative beingness then returns and again we carve words in an unstoppable, powerful flow like the Tennessee River. Unless I shut her out, grace always comes to my semi-bashful rescue sounding like laughter instead of tears. *"Oh, was that me thinking again? Let's stop this right now and turn it over to Grace . . ."*

Close travel companion to grace is the most trusted and faithful river guide of all existence: intuition. I choose to walk on intuition's strong bridge for almost everything, and I consider it a blessing to have such a natural bent for leaping before I look. I can always figure out what happened later. By the by, this mindset is hands down my open road to successful, joyful, creative writing and living. My intuitive style does come with a price, however. I have to live with the ten-headed perfectionist monster that busts in to censor me just as things seem too easy. I vividly recall many moments of instinctive highs quickly followed by heart crushing, doubtful lows. Who on earth did I think I was to be so bold and brave in the swift wind of inspiration, writing without a net? Now I know definitively that if I give up what the process is supposed to look like, I can expect wisdom and answers with every turn of phrase. What a powerful feeling!

After years of dry skies, I am grateful to report a steady shower of creative writing whenever I do the "I am" rain dance of universal law. I water my state of "I am creative" with reverence so I can get up and do it again tomorrow. I never want to go back to my writing days as Wild Bill and the Lone Ranger with a disregard for systems and support. Although my ego is more comfortable with me pretending to be a powerless child, I bravely choose to embrace my power, freedom, and grace every day, because that is who I came to be in the world. It is nothing less than my perfect natural order.

In closing, I graciously extend a personal invitation to adopt another gold-star transformation practice of mine: Go easy on your good self. Realize the ego is a mother grizzly bear, James Bond, and a Navy SEAL rolled into one whose sole job it is to keep your creative container small. If it's small you won't be able to receive as much. You need a bigger one than ego will provide you.

Put down the beat-up stick and pick up the plume pen of grace, which will tickle you gladly. Give way to your inner-authority who is certain of your beingness as power and freedom.

Consider that each of us feels a bit scared when stepping into the current of abundance. After all, society conditions us for lack and not enough. Do I really deserve all this word flow? Yes! Take the luxury cruise ship of inspiration and ditch the flimsy life raft. Keep choosing your power; you deserve it. Because it will sail you around the ego's bank and into a crystal deep-blue pool of creative waters, beckoning you to take a dip. Why not shed your modesty and have wild, skinny-dipping fun with your writing? You just might allow yourself to emerge refreshed and changed forever.

Enjoy your swim.

The Soul and Creativity

Meg Haworth, Ph.D.

Walk into any bookstore and you will be surrounded by the passion of writers who placed their soulful expressions upon the pages of their books. As you peruse the shelves, stop for a moment and sense the lives of these sojourners of the written word. The books of poetry, prose, plays, fiction, puzzles, biography, photography, reference, and guidance all around you were created by teams of people committed to manifesting the vision of one (or sometimes more) writing souls into tangible printed pieces of creativity.

You cannot move one inch on this planet called Earth without bumping up against creation. The sidewalk you walk upon, the building you peer up at, the computer you communicate through, the butterfly floating by you, the tiny blades of grass—all things are created by somebody (or something) somewhere. As humans, we have an enormous capacity for creation. We are constantly manifesting our thoughts and feelings in creative forms by virtue of an inescapable force called free will. We all have free will to create.

As a spiritual healer and counselor, transpersonal therapist, radio show host, and author, my nature requires me to create. I cannot live without it. From morning to night and into my dream state, I create constantly—and I assert that do you, too. We are all creating something. We live in the energy of creation without end at all times. That is our very being. But what are you creating? Are you creating the day you want? Are you composing the song within your heart or creating a sculptural masterpiece or drafting a penetrating business newsletter? I guarantee you are creating something.

So many of us associate creativity with artistic expression alone. It is as if we believe you have to be a musician, painter, singer, performer, writer, or another kind of artist to be considered a creative person. This is simply not the truth. Creativity comes in all forms. You may think that an accountant is not creative, but how is it not creative to form a budget, assist a client to receive a tax break, or come up with a new strategy to stretch a tiny income? It begs the question: In what form does your creativity come?

Look at your life. Through your actions and words you may be creating fear, sadness, turmoil, and pain for yourself or for others. You may think you have no choice in the matter. Perhaps you believe that your parents acted and spoke this way and so must you, as you claim, "That is all I know." Maybe you think that you cannot change—or perhaps you are afraid to change. Be honest with what you create on a daily basis. You may be creating a life of pain when instead you could have a life of joy and greatness.

You may complain that you are trying but rationalize that you just cannot create because you have writer's block, or a terminal disease, or you were abused as a child. Perhaps you cannot concentrate because you're entirely too stressed out right now from the demands of your life. Think about this: You created the stress, the fear, the writer's block, the excuses of a bad childhood or a stressed life. Could you create differently?

Are your hackles up? Good.

The fears that you create are often the very thing standing in the way of your greatest creations. If you can brilliantly create fear, sorrow, pain, and stress, then you can brilliantly create joy, happiness, love, and fun, too. You are *that* powerful. When you create from joy, then you bring things to the world that reflect joy.

Many people transmute sorrow and pain through creativity. Listen to just about any country song and you will feel it. Perhaps you also are called to create from those emotions. If you are—and there are many artists, engineers, teachers, and the like who are— then create from that source. Use any emotion you desire as a catalyst to bring what you want to create into the world. Creativity is a healing force.

If you feel these painful emotions are standing in the way of your creativity, then find a great therapist who can help you clear them away so you can unblock your creative life force. The point is: You are in charge. You are the creator. You make the decisions to say yes or no to the creative force that is available to you. We all do.

If you feel as if you have not accessed your creativity since you were a child drawing sidewalk chalk art, singing in a choir, or writing a poem, you are not alone. So many adults feel as though they are not creative anymore. They feel the daily pulses of their lives are so rapid that in the process of just trying to keep up and make ends meet their creativity seems to elude them. You may believe you have no time to be creative. It is difficult even to access the desire to create when you may be working hard to get by. Within this scenario, creativity is perhaps needed most.

In my program *Earth School: Life Lessons from Your Soul*, I teach the differences between the personality and the soul in an effort to help people everywhere understand how to create using the most powerful partner, healer, friend, and creative force we have available to us: the soul. When our personalities connect with the power and wisdom of the soul, we have the potential to create anything we truly desire. It is in uniting with this permanent force that we can become immortal here on Earth. We do this by leaving something behind of lasting value through what we create.

A key element in creation is desire. Our personalities must have the desire and the raw ability to create something lasting. Talent is useful in creation but not essential. Often a person can work to develop a skill that he or she has the deep desire to develop. The energy of desire is an electrical current of the soul that runs through the personality and fuels the project at hand. Desire is a force often coupled with passion. When these two electric forces combine, a feeling of being unstoppable kicks in. It is in this feeling that the super-human force of the soul works through the personality to create.

So often when an idea comes to you for creation, it comes in a quiet moment, such as in the shower, in the car, or on your daily run. When it does come to you, simply let it in. Jot it down somewhere so you won't forget it. You may not bring this idea to fruition for years to come, but now the seed has been planted. You may feel a sense of urgency to get it out as soon as possible. Feel it. Feel the strength of the desire and know that it will come into being when you have all the pieces you need to be able to deliver the idea to whomever it may be intended for. All creative projects come in as a thought first that we call an idea. Many of those creative thoughts need time to gestate and develop into the beautiful strong tree that grows from that seed thought.

William Shakespeare was one of the greatest writing personalities ever to walk the planet. I can only imagine the power that coursed through his being to create with the brilliance he did. I imagine that his characters lived within his mind, playing out their tragedies, comedies, love stories, and suspenseful plots with full fervor as they made their way to the page. His work has endured for over 500 years, and it continues to be played out on the stage and in motion pictures. No matter how his life may have been lived, no one can argue that the soul of his creativity has left an indelible mark upon our world.

There are countless examples of souls that generate and create in a myriad of ways. Oprah Winfrey is a master creator who brings education, entertainment, enlightenment, and prosperity to her guests and her worldwide audiences. She is a highly creative personality who follows the directives of her soul by flowing her ideas out to her staff who make all these ideas happen. She is an example of someone who takes action to create through her soul's expression. She is not painting sweeping murals or writing epic screenplays. Nonetheless, she is in constant creation, raising the consciousness of humanity and seeming to be having a lot of fun in the process.

The soul of creativity lives within each person. We all cannot be William Shakespeare or Oprah Winfrey—only they could fill those roles—but each of us has access to the same creative force, and we can be ourselves. We can access passion, desire, excitement, joy, love, peace, hope, faith, and all the other forces it takes for each us to create in just the way we are led. The personality only needs to choose how to create through its spiritually granted power of free will. Your free will to choose may well be the greatest power you have. So what are you going to create today?

Is there something you loved to do as a child? Maybe you loved to write, sing, dance, sew, compute, take things apart and put them back together again, draw, sculpt, garden, cook, play sports, play an instrument, film home movies, or act. Think about the things you loved and did for the sheer enjoyment of doing them. You may not have been truly great at that activity, but I bet you loved it anyway. So often as children we are encouraged to create, but then, as we get older, we begin to compare our work to others or we are criticized for not being the best. Often we compare ourselves right out of doing the very thing with which we might have creatively contributed to this planet.

Just take a moment to think about what you loved to do as a child. Close your eyes for a moment and see yourself doing that thing you loved. Maybe you can picture a drawing you once drew, reciting a poem you wrote, or playing a song you used to play on the piano.

How did it feel to do that thing? Feel the sense of enjoyment or excitement or calming run through you as you think of your childhood creations.

What might you like to begin to do again? Is there something you have always wanted to try? Begin to think about creating from a different place other than the stress of your daily life or your fears or sadness—unless those emotions are your creative catalyst. Begin to think about creating from enjoyment, passion, desire, and fire.

If there is something you have always wanted to do, begin to do it now. Take one step towards it right now. Pick up a pencil and begin to draw on printer paper. You do not have to buy out the supplies in your local arts store. You can start small and begin to create the thing that makes you feel alive. Use your free will to create that one step, and then create the next one. Houses are built foundation first.

You may have a solid talent already lying in wait within you. Access it. You may have a great book in you or a song that everyone needs to dance to or sing. Take the tiniest step of giving yourself permission to create from your joy and excitement rather than your stress and fear. After you take your tiny step forward, start thinking about setting a bigger goal, like writing a book or having three new poems completed by the end of the month, or signing up for piano or dance lessons. Find a community theater to get involved in or volunteer for storytelling time at your local library.

And if you feel blocked when you begin, that's okay. Keep going.

I worked with a client who regularly participates in triathlons. He says that every time he stands on the shore of the Pacific Ocean to begin the swimming portion, he becomes overwhelmed for a brief moment. He looks at the massive ocean and remembers the strategy he uses to get out past the breakwaters. He knows that once he jumps in the ocean and begins the process it is a very short trip to finding his flow. He is then already participating in the moment, moving along through the water, as he completes the distance he set out to do.

Like this athlete, when you commit to a creative project, it works much the same way. Once you begin and find the flow of the paint brush, the lilt of the tune, the shapely woman in the clay, the pattern in the mosaic, the grain of the wood, the arch in the doorway, the speech you will deliver, the mathematical equation, or any other flow you may find within what ever you create, you are ready to bring your specific expression to the world. Flow is the natural expression of your soul working through your personality to bring in your desire, your unique contribution. You are the only one who can create like you do. Just choose to begin.

Once you have taken the first step, here are some things you can do to focus on creating the opening for your flow to happen:

1. Close your eyes and take three deep breaths in through the nose and out through the mouth. Simply quieting your inner dialogue with your breath can begin to put you in touch with your creative soul.
2. Speak an intention aloud for what you want to create: "I intend for my soul to offer a song to me today that I may share with the world" or, "I

intend to write one chapter of my book today, and I ask that it be given to me easily and effortlessly."
3. Now, focus on the in-breath and the out-breath. Notice how peaceful you become as you focus. Allow any words, images, thoughts, or ideas to come to you to get started.
4. Now go to the canvass, the computer, the business plan, or the river—wherever you go to create your soulful work.

When you get quiet and intentionally connect with the inspiration of the soul, you can access the best of your creativity. Just focus your attention and allow the flow of creative soul current to guide you. There is a tremendous power in the stillness of your mind and the flow of your breath. The life force of the soul can come through more easily in stillness. You may feel great passion, fire, and motivation carrying you through the doing part of your creation, but if you are still it is born of the peace of the soul.

I worked with a woman who had many talents. She could sing and dance, and write poetry, essays, and songs. She could draw beautiful pictures and she had a knack for spreading love everywhere she went. But she hid her talents. She felt fearful, sad, confused, doubtful, ashamed, and embarrassed most of the time. She was brilliant at covering up her pain. Unfortunately for her, covering her pain meant that her talents remained hidden as well. Hiding is what she knew how to do.

The more she hid the more her soul attempted to awaken her personality to her greater gifts. As her personality continued to choose to hide, using her free will to do so, her soul continued to lead her to experiences that it hoped would awaken her. She became ill. She developed multiple stress-related disorders. She was inundated with sleep disturbances at night and physical, emotional, and mental discomfort during the day. She had poor relationships. She had an overall outlook that was hopeless, shameful, sorrowful and plagued with insecurities. She did not want to be on Earth if it meant suffering was a part of her daily routine.

One day it all changed. She had a realization that she had to do something different or she would be doomed to a life of pain. She got help. She cleared away the trauma of past abuses that she dwelled in every day. She committed to her healing and asked her soul to join her on the journey of her life. As hard as it was for her personality to jump out of the driver's seat of her life, she knew that she did not like the scenery on that dark and bumpy ride. She began to let the soul do its work to fix the vehicle of her life—her physical body, mental health, and emotional state. And she began to awaken the spiritual within her. Her soul healed her and her creative life force began to course through her with great power and love.

Today, she is an author, a healer, a teacher, a speaker, a poet, a songwriter, a singer, an artist, and a lover of life. Today, she is writing this essay for this book.

If you identify with my story, I pray you make a decision to change your life right here and right now. Commit to the beautiful soul you are and allow *your* unique expression to come through you. Do not deny the world of your song, your book, your accounting firm, your engineering breakthrough, your painting, your teaching skills, your activism, your individual *soul-ular* expression. You are a great being who came here from the source of all greatness. Connect with the infinite glory of your soul and bring through your contribution. Don't worry about who is going to like it. Just know that you will leave it behind for others to take from it what they will.

You are a great creator. Find what you desire to create. When you do, you become who you are—a creator of love and life. Just be that.

Five Creative Benefits of the Conscious Use of Voice and Music

Eliana Gilad

Sound is everywhere. Music is sound. Your voice is sound.

Vibration is the first physical manifestation of pure. All matter vibrates, from the densest rock to the faintest wisp of smoke, and thus produces sound. The nucleus of every atom vibrates. Although sound waves are invisible, they can be sculpted as they pass through material objects, such as the skin of a drum, the strings of a harp, or through the vocal cords. Voice is the most intimate human instrument, which is why song can move us so deeply. It is also why many people are sensitive regarding their voices, whether related to singing or the spoken word.

Do you sometimes find yourself intending to communicate one thing, yet actually saying something else? Is your silent inner voice attuned to your outer physical voice? Do blocks get in the way of your expression? Your voice bridges your inner and outer worlds, and thus it has the power to transform your life if you use it skillfully. Approaching your voice as you would a musical instrument can help you increase the amount of peace and harmony in your daily life. Learning to use your voice consciously is a wise investment that will provide you multiple dividends.

Try this exercise to tune into your own body instrument.

Imagine yourself on a crowded urban street. Imagine horns honking, machinery humming, sirens blaring, and vehicles passing. You are hearing a cacophony of sound.

Now imagine yourself walking by the ocean on a windy day. Imagine waves crashing, the tide moving in and out, loose, dry sand being blown about and skittering along packed, wet sand, and seagulls crying above you in the sky.

Both scenes are filled with strong sounds. Yet their effects upon your mind, body, and soul would be quite different. Unconsciously heard urban sounds typically strain and tire people, while natural sounds typically relax and energize people. How they are affected depends upon where they focus. The more people are aware of their focus, the more easily they can create an environment that's to their liking.

Sound waves carry the energy of the people creating them. When angry and stressed, the vibration transmitted to listeners will be tense. When relaxed and calm, the resulting tones will be harmonious. By taking a moment to listen to the inner tone of your voice prior to speaking, you can tune your instrument to bring forth a peaceful tone that creates healthier connections and more fulfilling communication.

The Voices of Eden method of speaking and singing that I created and teach to individuals and groups is based upon the conscious use of sound and rhythm as natural healing instruments, a practice that dates back to ancient matriarchal times. In those days, voice, rhythm (in the form of drumming and dance), and music were routinely used for healing and spiritual purposes. They still are used today in these ways, yet in very different forms. For example, ultrasound is the medical application of sound to measure tissue density. The vibratory rate of sounds waves passing through thicker and thinner soft tissue is translated into pictures we can see on a computer screen.

In Voices of Eden music, the ancient sound practices are applied to modern purposes. For example, wordless vocals are combined with pre-biblical percussion instruments to bypass the intellect and connect listeners to their inner cores. No electronic synthesizers are used, so it's as if the listeners are being "fed" the full "vitamins" of the notes with no "preservatives."

Here are five major benefits of consciously using music and your voice to stimulate, facilitate, and accelerate your creative process.

1. **Reduced Stress.** One of my clients, a food additive manufacturer, puts recorded healing music to good use in a variety of ways. The company originally purchased 1,000 Voices of Eden CDs to give away as a small gift of appreciation to its clients and suppliers. The all-natural, no-additive music reinforced their public reputation as a company that produces high-quality, environmentally friendly products. The company received such positive reports from its clients (whose staff members reported experiencing less stress, more joy, and having increased focus on the job when the music was being quietly played in the background) that they decided to provide the music to their own employees as well.

   In your own life, playing wordless vocal healing music in the background while you create can reduce the pressure. Here is a tip you can use to turn commuting time into prime relaxed creative time (while even staying alert at the wheel). Instead of tuning into the news or a commercial radio station, play a CD on low volume while you hold in mind the experience you would *like* to have during the day (or evening, if it is at the end of the day). Notice the pattern of your breathing change with the rhythm of the percussion instruments. If the desire arises to spontaneously speak or sing out . . . go ahead! The power of your voice will energize and relax you at the same time.

2. **Increased Creative Flow.** The former mayor of the city of Safed, Israel, recognized as the birthplace of Jewish mysticism, has develop-

ed a unique local tour in which he guides groups through the alleyways of his ancient town while singing about its history through famous songs written about it. The combination of his prominence and his singing tour contributes in a true and genuine way to preserving the history of his nation and of Safed's spiritual community. After studying and incorporating the five elements of the Voices of Eden approach in his programs, the Mayor demonstrates the power of ingeniously weaving together his natural voice and life experiences to contribute towards the creation of a more harmonious world.

In your own life, draw upon the conscious use of rhythm and voice to enhance your creative flow by noticing your individual way of communicating. Notice the particular ways in which you use words to express yourself and consciously exaggerate it. It may amuse you and spur greater creativity. For example, once, while waiting for a train I interrupted a conversation to say I wanted to "plant myself," pointing with my finger to the exact location "over there" where I intended to board the arriving train. I hopped into the spot and announced, "There, now I am planted. So you were saying?" My friend was amused.

3. **Improved Performance.** One of my clients, a professional singer, came to me to connect with the 90 percent of her voice that never seemed to come out when she was up on the stage. "Everyone else says I have a beautiful voice," she told me, but she wanted to be able to connect with this "other voice" and give more of herself on stage so she

could truly make a mark with a special message. Through implementing the relaxation and focusing exercises of the Voices of Eden approach to consciously use her voice as an instrument, she reported being able to remain focused on her artistry and on communicating the essence of the music to the audience when she sang. Concerts now bring her more pleasure than they formerly did, and she worries less about how well she is performing. Recently, she received three prestigious invitations to perform overseas with other internationally renowned singers in her field. Her exposure has grown exponentially.

In your own life, focus upon where you are feeling most at ease and excited when you are performing. When you identify that place, dive into it even more. Keep your focus there. It does not matter whether you are singing or speaking or making a presentation. The same approach applies to all three and will bring you added pleasure and enjoyment. Your listeners will be more inspired as well.

4. ***Increased Confidence.*** For people who use their voices a lot in the course of doing their work, such as teachers, lecturers, attorneys, and those in service industries, conscious use of voice can make a marked difference upon the quality of work and communication with others. Yves, a senior sales executive for a high-tech company, decided to apply the conscious vocal tools he had learned in an eight-week vocal healing course I gave to overcome fear and increase his confidence. His habit was to meet with 20 prospective customers

each week, closing a sale once every three to four weeks. In the midst of the course, he decided to cut the number of his weekly sales visits down to five and to visit the prospective clients that scared him most. This was his way to practice the exercise of letting go of the blocks that stood in the way of using his natural voice with ease. That week his sales quadrupled. Yves attributed his new success to his increased ability to focus, which improved his inner calm and bolstered his confidence, allowing him to connect authentically with his prospects and thereby increasing his sales results drastically.

In your own life, is there is some area of your creative process that causes you anxiety or where you do not yet feel as if you are certain you have the ability to succeed? If so, try this . . . Give yourself permission to take one small portion of the process and "mess it up." Usually, when you are willing to do it all wrong, many wonderful surprises await you on the other side.

5. *Team Building.* In ancient times, music was a sacred art meant to connect the listener to the source of all creation. Both the musician and the listener were necessary for a given sound's power to be activated. A modern application of sound teaches a pleasurable and fun way to increasing listening skills, giving and receiving, listening and being heard while increasing cooperation between different kinds of people. For example, the ancient practice of call and response is an excellent means to open up the creative flow and healthy communication process among the members of a

group. One person begins by spontaneously saying or singing a word, the rest of the group mirrors it vocally. Listening is enhanced as the "choir" members focus upon what the leader says or sings.

In your own life, look for the ways in which you can "take the ball" from someone else by repeating what you heard before adding your own flavor to the message.

Having learned these five creative benefits of the conscious use of voice and music, you can now add this additional dimension into your creative process. Whatever type of creative process you are involved in, the conscious use of voice and music can help you tap into the deep well of your own inspiration. These tools work for anyone, not just singers and professional speakers or presenters. You are truly an instrument, and your voice matters. How you use it makes a difference in the world. What kind of music will your unique notes create?

Creativity Is Life

Elaine Springer

Creativity is the force that keeps me alive. What are we if not a result of creation? One of the fundamental unsolved mysteries of mankind is the origin of our existence. We still have no proof or agreement on this subject. Creation is infinite and ever changing. If not for creation, I would not be able to write these words.

An ongoing question for me in my life has always been, "What am I doing here?" I am always searching for meaning and find great joy in the interconnectedness of all things. Here are a few things I know about life:

I know I feel best when I am in the company of harmony and love.

I seek to create by staying connected to my soul. I know I am connected when I feel love and a sense of union with myself, with another person, with the words of a song, or an image in a painting, or a line in a book.

I love bringing people together for the sake of making life easier and more joyous for all those concerned. Helping another person brings a smile to my face and puts a warm feeling in my heart.

At this point in my life I have come to believe that our true essence is love.

When we operate from this level of consciousness, we feel good because we are being true to our true selves. In reality we are all one. When we do something to harm or undermine another, we feel bad because we are really doing something destructive to our own selves. We are off-center.

Human beings have the possibility to think and act and feel the result of their thoughts and actions. All suffering could be mitigated by operating from the truth of the nature of things. Be good to yourself and treat others as you want to be treated and then your life will be grand!

Art is a magnificent mode of expression because it allows us to share the pain we feel inside without directly harming a fellow human being. Personally I would rather experience pain through gazing at a painting or a piece of art than experience its onslaught in person through the words or actions of a fellow human being. Therefore, I salute artistic expression for giving us this outlet.

Because I know I am my consciousness, and what I put into my mind contributes to my own self-creation, I try to fill my life with works of art that uplift my spirit. A flower, a bee, a warm smile, a compliment, an opening, a space to be myself and to be engaged in a heart-to-heart conversation with another person make my life worth living. Art has given me the possibility to express all aspects of my being in harmony. Harmony is the key—I feel at peace and vibrantly alive simultaneously.

We do have the power to create our lives exactly how we would like them to be. This requires looking at ourselves, and seeking help and advice, and it ultimately brings us into communion with like-minded individuals. We get to experience the joy of authenticity amongst our friends. Although this frequently requires a leap of faith and courage, it is well worth it.

What continually amazes me is the expanse of the creative spirit. I recently became an active participant of the professional networking website called LinkedIn. Through my connections there I was subsequently invited to be a friend on Facebook. I am having a blast dialoguing electronically. The opportunities for creating and learning through social media such as these with "strangers" worldwide has astounded me and warms my heart. In short, it has given me access to new universes without even leaving my apartment.

But leave my apartment, I must. Being creative in nature I find that sometimes I can get too caught up in my mind and self, and then I end up feeling drained. Always I must remember the importance of maintaining balance in life.

Discipline and awareness are vital aspects of creation. Without them, we can become lost in the vastness of the cosmos. I have had that experience and now have returned to find balance. Life always is a balancing act. Writing a bit, emailing a lot, eating, exercising, thinking, meditating, praying, taking care of those in need, watering the plants, and driving the car while maintaining connection to my soul throughout all of it. Staying connected to my soul has enabled me to survive an array of abuses that I have been subjected to since birth.

Having the seed of abuse in my consciousness caused me to experience it in every form, from my family of origin, peers, friends, spouse, employers, lovers, and, yes, even and especially from my spiritual teachers. I work daily to heal this aspect of myself and share this information with the intention of helping others do the same. I have emerged from silence to fearless self-expression, and I feel eternally grateful.

My life and my work are dedicated to the pursuit of aiding the perpetrators and recipients of abuse in their mutual recoveries. In reality they are lovers—one cannot exist without the other. Compassion and connecting to the pain of the abuser had taught me a great deal about human behavior and the powerlessness and insecurity an abuser must feel unconsciously when engaged in putting down another. That is what binds abusers and victims: a sense of powerlessness, fear, and insecurity. I work to fill this space with compassion, love, understanding, and the knowledge that nothing can destroy my true self.

My true self is my soul. My life force is eternal and knows that every time I choose compassion, I gain spiritual strength and the power to succeed and help others do the same. The world needs to know peace. We need to trust each other and move on and evolve past our history. This is the meaning of life for me.

May we create with compassion and find the wisdom and strength to keep our destructive natures confined to board games and artistic expression.

Beauty and Fear

Dr. Beatrice Kraemer

Have you ever experienced being told that you have nothing to offer the world? I had the opportunity to hear that once from a former boyfriend of mine. How do you suppose that would make you feel? It made me feel like shit. But what is even more interesting to me, in retrospect as a psychologist and as someone who on most days feels damn good about herself, was the range of responses that I had at the time. They went from, "You idiot, you don't even know me" and, "No, that can't be true!" to, "Wow, he may be right." Of course, today I know it did not matter at all what this man thought of my worth and my ability to create value for others. What mattered was that his feedback served as a trigger for me to look inside myself to find out why the comment bothered me so much.

And so I did. Gradually, through a process of self-reflection, what I found was: He was both right and wrong. There was much that I had to offer to the world. I could feel it! Yet I just did not know what exactly it was or how to bring it out of me.

So there I was, in my early 40s, having basically the same problem I'd always had: I thought what I had to say was not a useful contribution. I decided it was not good enough and just had to be better. It seems as if there has always been a denigrating voice inside me telling me that what I have to offer never will live up to the standards that somebody else has set for me or that I made up for myself, for whatever reason. This voice has been with me since I was able to think—and probably even before then.

My fear that was triggered by my boyfriend's comment was twofold. For one, I was literally afraid that what I would find inside me did not match some mysterious standard. I was afraid of being myself. Secondly, on a larger scale but perhaps equally as important, I could not fathom that who and what I was would actually be something that people would want, could use, and might even seek out. Even if I admitted that I liked myself and who I was, what if other people still thought there was nothing valuable in me, nothing that would contribute to their well being?

So there it is, the beauty and the fear were the same thing. I wanted to be and admire who I was, but I was afraid that people would tear me down. I could not make a contribution without risking failure, and I was a failure if I didn't contribute.

As a therapist working mostly with eating disordered patients, I have noticed this confusing mechanism over and over again of letting something outside dictate their inner experience. In patients with these disorders, you find a lack of self-awareness and self-definition, as well as a lack of boundaries, self-esteem, and self-confidence. They follow internalized voices that are not theirs telling them what to do and what not to do. They are big into should's and should-not's. It was ironic that I had been trained to accompany my patients on their journeys to find out who they are and what they have to offer, yet I had not traveled that journey myself, or at least not gone to the fullest extent possible with it.

I realized that to change this mechanism for me would take a few elements. First, I needed to be willing to change it. Otherwise, my mind would trick me and would find a way to stick to the old pattern. So I had to make a conscious decision to find out who I was and what I had to offer. I intentionally committed myself to creating myself.

A second element needed in the process was courage. It is much easier to be mad at your ex-boyfriend (or your parents or teacher or boss, for that matter) for telling you nasty things, but not as easy to see that it is actually you who is putting the limits on you. However, the part that takes the most courage is to change the mechanism of letting them define who you are and how much that is worth. Changing may mean that, while you are letting go of some old patterns and re-creating your world, you just won't know how life will be and where it will lead. This brings up the prospect of beauty and fear again.

A third important element in the process is paying attention. When I realized that my ex-boyfriend was simply personifying my internal voice, I also realized that I had probably chosen him for that exact reason. Like me, he was big into "shoulds."

Once I understood, I looked around in my world and noticed all those moments, situations, and places in which I put myself, and noticed all the people whose company I sought out that were matching the internal voice that prevented me from being creative and exercising my talents. It took a while and also some pain to put myself in different types of situations where I could hang out with people who are more validating, put fewer expectations on me, and let me be just who I am at any moment in time.

Another part of any healing process is learning to pay attention to how you select information. If five people gave me positive feedback and five people gave me negative feedback, then earlier, I promise, I would have chosen to hear the negative feedback *only*. Let me be honest, I still listen to negative feedback, but today I am much more free to evaluate the feedback for what it is and I decide if, and how, I will integrate it. But what is even more important is that I *also* listen to the positive feedback and integrate it. Doing anything creative is a dynamic and enjoyable process

Beauty and Fear 225

as I can literally feel how, by virtue of this process, the voices inside change and it unblocks the flow of creativity.

There is one last element that I find important: curiosity. At times, it feels quite scary not to know exactly where you are going and if, in the end, you will be fine. But I have learned to let curiosity be the friend of fear, because it is fascinating to experience the unknown, to be like a child that encounters so many new things to explore. And there is one amazing thing: the more I practice being curious, the bigger my curiosity gets. The voice of this curiosity, in quite a funny way, asks, "What if?" Whereas before I almost always had a clear idea of what constitutes "worthwhile," now I let that curious little voice guide me and I trust it. Let me give you an example.

I teach at a university. In the beginning, I was so scared of not being the "right" teacher, of not explaining things "properly," of not choosing the "right" reading, of not being "stimulating and interesting," and of not being "creative enough" to be able to get the students interested and engaged in the topic at hand. I took this fear so far that, in the end, I felt fairly suffocated and was not even sure anymore if I understood my topics correctly myself. But since I had committed myself to teaching these classes, I had no choice other than to go into the classroom and to do and to be. What helped me was that I asked myself, "What if it works?" The minute I asked that question, a smile would appear on my face. I could sense that it might actually work. It opened up a possibility. So I went into the classroom and acted "as if" I was myself, "as if" I was a person who was witty enough to give good examples, "as if" I was personable and creative. It took me five minutes, and then I was myself. I had managed to trick myself into being myself.

So when I think of creating now, this is how I encourage myself.

I invite you to do the same.

For the Love of It

―――――――――

Jeff Fasano

So, I am on the number 1 train headed to the gym after a long day at a job I truly hate. Sitting alone surrounded by many glum nine-to-fivers, who probably disliked their jobs as much as I did mine, an image from my not so distant past pops into my head: the face of Terry, a woman with whom I'd had a relationship. I could hear her voice. When we decided to break it off, one of the many things she said was, "Jeff, I love you, but you hate your job and your life. The only time you're happy is when you are with me."

Hearing her comment again was like the scene in *Moonstruck* when Cher slaps Nicholas Cage across the face and says, "Snap out of it!"

Terry's voice jarred me. It got my attention. At that moment I realized that she'd been right. I did hate my job. I wasn't keen about where I was with my life. And I knew I had to do something about it. Instead of going to the gym that night, I went straight home.

When I got there, I changed out of the suit and tie that I detested wearing and grabbed a yellow legal pad. At the top of the pad I wrote: "What do I want to be when I grow up?"

I was 33 years old and it was 1994.

Well, I sat there and looked at the blank page for a minute. Then I closed my eyes and asked myself: What could I do that I am good at? I started writing things down, many crazy things, too many to even remember, and among those many noble professions, I wrote down photography. I know I went to college for some reason, but I am not sure of what except to get a degree. In 1980 that was the pre-requisite to higher advancement. As I looked over that list of a bunch of very safe things I could do, my eyes kept coming back to photography, which was definitely not safe, in my opinion.

I'll digress a bit here. In 1988, a friend suggested that since I loved photography so much I ought to take a class at Parsons. That suggestion resonated with me and I enrolled. At Parson's I met Mario Cabrera, an amazing man who taught me the craft. I spent two years with him, loving every minute of it. I took three different photography classes over the next three years and had fun shooting pictures all over New York City. Then I met Terry. Because I would photograph her often, I realized I loved doing it. I decided to take one more class in order to learn about portraiture and lighting.

Cutting to the chase, Terry encouraged me regarding my talent and even prophesized one day that I'd end up with a career as a photographer, saying, "What am I going to do when you are shooting beautiful models for *Vogue*?" I thought she was nuts, but as we move along with this story, you'll see she wasn't very far off.

Okay, back to the story.

I am back looking at my list and photography calls my attention. I decide to put the pad down and get something to eat. "I'll come back to this." When I did, an hour later, I read over everything I had written down again and again photography called to me. Back then, I wasn't into meditation, but I sat back and closed my eyes, took a deep breath, and—in the silence—it hit me: I *loved* making photographs. The feeling was so strong that the moment I realized this, I suddenly sat up and opened my eyes. *Taking pictures is one of the most joyful experiences I've ever had!* Right then and there, I committed to being a photographer.

The next morning was the beginning of the rest of my life.

I dedicated my life to doing photography. With financial help from my father, I bought lights and transformed my kitchen into a darkroom and my living room into a photo studio. I set up my lights, put up backgrounds, and shot any beautiful woman who was willing, as well as friends, male and female, who would care to be shot.

I would create setups and shoot on weekends, and sometimes on weeknights, and then I'd have the film processed and print the images at night, sometimes staying awake until three in the morning. Then I'd get up the next day and wash and dry the prints. All this work was leading me towards building a portfolio.

I was still working at my job, the one that I hated, but now I had something in my life that I'd never had before: passion. I was so passionate about making photographs that I spent my lunch hour almost every day shooting around downtown Manhattan near my office in the World Trade Center. I carried my camera everywhere I went, shooting and then printing what I shot, all in black and white. Being the great teacher and mentor that he is, Mario would get together with me, critique my work, and encourage me.

When I wasn't shooting in my living room studio, I created projects for myself. I did one called "The Homeless Project." For about three years, I went around New York City shooting portraits of homeless men and women. The project continued until I couldn't do it emotionally any more. I was proud when those images were included in a group show.

My commitment was to learn everything I could about the craft of photography. Integrity was important to me. If I was to do this as my profession, I needed to be ready to do anything a potential client would ask me and pay me to do. So I studied the works of the masters: Eugene Smith, Walker Evans, and Dorothea Lange. As time went on, I also began to meet other photographers and professionals in the business that guided me to move forward with what I now realized was a dream. They told me I could live the dream if I remained committed and kept shooting.

Still living in a nine-to-five world, I slowly became more and more irritated. One day in an impulsive mood, I said to my father, "I need to quit this job." He told me that I wasn't ready to, but that I would know exactly when I was ready because I would feel it. "You will know when it is time," he said. I thought about the comment he made and decided to begin saving money, enough so that when I was ready to quit I'd have enough to live for a year. I made a plan. I also began taking the portfolio that I had built around town and showing it to magazines and modeling agencies. I knew it was pretty good. I began getting some nice reviews from those who saw it, and Mario kept on critiquing.

From showing my portfolio, I got some small jobs here and there. It was fun to make a bit of money doing what I loved to do. One day, my work friend Donna saw what I was doing and asked me what I really wanted to take pictures of. I said, "I want to shoot music." I love music, which really is an understatement. It is a staple in my life. It has inspired me ever since I grew up with it. "Well," Donna said, "I have a friend over at RCA Records."

"Can you hook me up?" I asked.

"Sure."

A couple of days later we went up to the RCA building in Times Square on our lunch hour and met her friend, Deb, who took my portfolio over to their art department. Deb came back and told me to come back in a day or so, but to call first. Two days later, I called and she told me to come pick up my book. When I got there, Deb said that the art director, Rich, wanted to meet me. I met him and we exchanged pleasantries. He told me he liked my work and I left. About three weeks later I got a call from Rich asking me if I'd like to go to Chicago and shoot James Galway for his next record.

Holy crap!

Of course, I accepted the gig. I used vacation time to go and do the shoot. It was an amazing experience. A friend had introduced me to another friend in Chicago, who had a studio I could use for the shoot, and off I went, nervous but very excited. Jimmy Galway was great to shoot. He and RCA loved the images, which they ultimately used for more than one record. I made thousands for the one shoot and saved it all. This was mid-1997.

Once I knew I could live my dream, I felt antsy to quit my office job and I disliked it even more. Now it felt as if I was compromising or somehow betraying myself. I have since come to realize that I was not living my soul's plan at the office. The life I was living was not in resonance with my soul's desires. But I hung on for another year, during which a few more small jobs came along and my bank account was building.

It was now October 1998. One day when I came back from lunch, it hit me. "Now is the time." I sat down and typed up a resignation letter effective at the end of the year and handed it to my boss. It felt perfect and natural. I knew it was time. My father was right.

December 31, 1998, was the last day of my "old" life. I would be 40 that March. Beginning my new life I was ecstatic, nervous, and uncertain, yet it all felt right at the same time and I had no question that I made the right decision. I still remember waking up that first Monday morning not having to go to work like I had for 18 years. Wow!

Well, New Year's Eve rolled around. A photo lab in town was having a meet-and-greet party where photographers and people in the business could connect. Among other people, I met Tommy Saint, who looked at my portfolio and told me I should shoot fashion. He said, "You have the chops. You know lighting. All you have to do is put beautiful women in the place of the homeless people." I'd never given fashion a thought until then. But I went and found a book of photographs by Peter Lindbergh and studied his fashion photography.

I began going to modeling agencies with my portfolio in order to "test" their models and build a book. This way I had free access to models and they had free access to a photographer. I did lots of testing, met many models, stylists, and makeup artists, and built a great book in the process. Shooting portraits in my living room studio and doing an occasional job here and there comprised most of my year's activities in 1999.

The year 2000 came, the turn of the century. I continued testing and doing the occasional small job. One day in February I met a makeup artist, an amazing woman named Maria who had just moved to New York from Los Angeles. Unbeknownst to me, meeting Maria would change my life. She became my primary makeup and hair stylist, and a friendship began to grow. We did many shoots together. On one particular shoot she introduced me to a model, Alexandra, with whom I immediately connected. Alex in turn introduced me to her healer, Robert Baker, who was changing her life spiritually.

Even though I was now pursuing my passion for photography, I knew something was still missing in my life. When Alex gave me Robert's information, I jumped at the chance to see him. Just like I knew that I had to leave my job, the same happened with Robert; I knew I had to work with him. Our healing sessions changed my life so profoundly that I began to know myself in a different way. Thus, I now looked at my passion, photography, differently, and its presence in my life began to grow more swiftly.

Soon I moved from testing models to getting jobs in the fashion world and doing campaigns for designers. My work was appearing in various magazine ads. This path culminated when I met a designer named Angel Sanchez, who asked me to do a ten-page story/shoot for him for Spanish *Vogue*.

Well Terry, you were right.

Fashion was my main photographic interest for the next three years. All the while I still felt my love for music and for doing portraits, but it took me a while to understand that I really didn't like the fashion world. What I love doing most is capturing the essence of someone's soul. This is not what I was doing shooting fashion.

During a conversation with my friend Stephanie, she asked me what I didn't like about my photo career. I said, "Fashion."

"Stop doing it," she advised." You can still have the same abundant career doing what you love doing."

That was the final key I needed in order to design my ideal career. I stopped doing fashion and haven't missed it one bit. Now I do what I do for the love of it. In the years following my decision, my focus has shifted to photographing artists: musicians, authors, actors, interior designers, dancers, fashion designers, and everyone else who is connected to a passion for bringing creative expression into the world. I began by shooting images regularly for magazines and for record packages for recording artists.

Through the magazine work, I cultivated connections and formed relationships that led me to exactly where I intended to be and what I intended to do as a photographer. Artists have many needs for photographs and I am someone who fulfills those needs. Fortunately, they also chose me to do their work. The resonance of being exposed to people who are living their lives and doing what they love at a high level of excellence took me to higher levels both as a photographer and in my personal life.

My life has changed in so many ways. I have had the opportunity to meet and work with wonderful people whom I've admired, seen in movies, heard on records, and read about in newspapers and magazines. I've traveled across the United States and all over the world doing photography. When a call for a photographer comes, I am ready to go. My main criterion is to undertake exciting projects that challenge me personally and professionally. As a result, I am rising to the top as a photographer.

My career today was only a dream ten years ago. I truly love what I do and who I have become. When I look back at my journey and what I have accomplished so far, first and foremost I feel gratitude for the commitment I made to myself and for those who have supported me along the way. There is so much more life to live now and so much more to give. It has been a long time since I heard Terry's voice and wondered what I was going to be when I grew up. The job I hated is a distant memory.

Soon I am turning 50. I feel as if am in the prime of my life with so much yet to do and see and feel. I am dedicated to live it and love it by being who I am with the same passion I discovered almost 15 years ago. I am living my dream!

Contributors

Richard Aronow, co-creator of The Great American Think Out, believes there is a universal intelligence that connects us all and with which (when we tap into it) we can create, be, and have all that we want—and more than we could possibly imagine. He is an entrepreneurial pioneer who has helped finance and owned many diverse investments across the United States in sectors such as retail, entertainment, advertising, real estate, alternative fuels, education, precious metals, energy, and technology. He is author of *Success in Just a Few Words* and has developed and sold over $300 million in products, including The Hollywood 48 Hour Miracle Diet, on TV and radio, in print, and through retail outlets. He is an owner and founder of American Clean Coal Fuels and Sunset Health Products, Inc. (a nutritional health company), and founder and CEO of Aronow Capital, LLC located in La Jolla, California, where he resides. Find out more at: **www.stopthinkingnow.com** and **www.richardaronow.com**.

Martine Bellen. After earning a graduate degree in creative writing at Brown University, Martine began working on the literary journal *Conjunctions*. For over ten years she was senior editor and is now a contributing editor. Martine started out in book publishing at Henry Holt and Company and then worked as an editor at Carroll & Graf Publishers. At these publishing houses she edited and acquired books by numerous successful authors, including

Denise Mina (she was the first to publish this award-winning crime writer in the U.S.), who is presently published by Little, Brown; the National Book Critics Circle Award winner Maureen Howard; and Amanda Filipacchi (author of *Nude Men, Vapor,* and *Love Creeps*). In 2001, Ms. Bellen went into business for herself as an independent editor and book doctor. Since that time, she has had the opportunity to work with established novelists and nonfiction writers, as well as emerging talent and innovative thinkers and professionals who are writing first books or book proposals. The books she has edited include *Magic Time* by Doug Marlette, *After Fidel* by Brian Latell, and *Harpsong* by Rilla Askew.

Martine is the author of six collections of poetry, including *The Vulnerability of Order* (Copper Canyon Press*); Tales of Murasaki and Other Poems* (Sun & Moon Press), which won the National Poetry Series Award; and *Places People Dare Not Enter* (Potes & Poets Press). She has written the libretto for *Ovidiana*, an opera based on Ovid's *Metamorphoses* (composer, Matthew Greenbaum) that has been performed in New York City and Philadelphia, and she is collaborating with the composer David Rosenboom on an opera based on the *Diamond Sutra*, entitled *Ah!* She has been a recipient of grants from the New York Foundation for the Arts, the Fund for Poetry, and won the American Academy of Poets Award. To find more information about Martine's literary services and poetry, visit her websites: **www.martinebellen.com** and **www.book doctor bellen.com**.

C. Russell Brumfield, author of *Whiff: The Revolution of Scent Communication in the Information Age*, is a classic entrepreneur with a keen ability to identify upcoming trends and to harness their potential. With an endless curiosity that is as diverse as his career, he is a student of science, technology, business, marketing, philosophy, religion, and metaphysics. His interests and experience have afforded him the insight to grasp the nature and potential of the pioneering field of scent communication. He is continually involved in new startup ventures and has built several multi-million dollar companies. His most notable venture has been Wizard Studios, an entertainment, event, and experiential design company catering to the Fortune 500. With clients like Chrysler, Lexus, Motorola, FedEx, Pfizer, Colgate, MTV, Disney, and the NFL, he became a trailblazer in the industry.

With business partner James Goldney, he founded Whiff Solutions, the world's leading scent marketing and branding company, providing leading edge companies with expertise and advice in the science, technology, and application of scent marketing and communication. Together with The Scent Marketing Institute, he established the annual Scent Marketing Expo and Conference.

Over the course of his career, Brumfield has conceived and honed many revolutionary concepts in his fields of endeavor. Now, with a laser focus on the amazing powers of scent, he has formulated new and exciting strategies and applications to benefit business and society. Delivering his message with clarity and wit, he is a sought-after speaker for international audiences and an entertaining teacher for seminars and workshops.

When he's not traveling, Brumfield spends his time in Clearwater Beach, Florida. You can visit him online at: **www.whiffbook.com** or **www.whiffsolutions.com**.

Paulette Callen was born in eastern South Dakota, graduated from Concordia College in Moorhead, MN, completed a year of graduate work in theatre at the University of Minnesota, and for ten years made her home in Minneapolis while she was active in small regional theatres. She moved to New York in 1977 where she studied acting and began writing. Her first written work was a play, *Angelique,* which enjoyed staged readings at the Apple Corps Theatre in Manhattan, and, a few years later, at the Attic Theatre in Jersey City, New Jersey.

Simon and Schuster published Callen's first novel, *Charity*, in 1997. The following year, Berkeley Signature brought out the paperback version. In 1994, she received the first-place award for fiction from Negative Capability Press in Mobile, Alabama. Her poems, stories, and essays have appeared in small journals and literary publications, most recently in *Tapestries* (October 2005) and previously: *Outerbridge*, *WOMANEWS, Horses All* (published in Canada), *Cats!*, and *The Animals' Voice*. She is a frequent contributor to *Between the Species: A Journal of Ethics* published by the Albert Schweitzer Foundation at Berkeley. Her poetry has been included in anthologies: *Women and Death* (Ground Torpedo

Press), *Cats' Meow* (Maine Rhoads), and *Beyond Lament: Poets of the World Bearing Witness to the Holocaust* (Northwestern University Press), from which the poem "See Nadia!" was selected by artist Carol Rosen for inclusion in her *Holocaust Series,* an eight-book collection of photo/text collages that has been displayed in the Whitney Museum (New York, NY), the Simon Wiesenthal Center in Los Angeles, California, and at the University of Tel Aviv (Israel).

Callen works in the communications department of a large corporation. She has been employed as a governess and has worked in a movie theatre, a bank, the gift industry, the ASPCA, and the insurance sector, as well as summer stock theatres and a yearlong stint with a comedy improvisation company. For four years she served as a staff member for POWARS (Pet Owners with AIDS Resource Services) in New York City. She lives with a rescued blind Shih Tzu on Manhattan's Upper West Side.

Accomplished entrepreneur, **Ernest D. Chu** has been a spiritual teacher for the past decade. Prior to that, he had a distinguished 30-year career in finance and investment, including as an allied member of the New York Stock Exchange, an investment-banking executive, and a capital markets expert. He has advised some of America's largest companies and has raised capital for hundreds of public- and private-growth companies in a variety of industries (**www.ernest chu.com**).

As an entrepreneur, he funded or was a member of the founding executive team of nine companies, three of which went public. He has raised more than $150 million for these and other client companies, and he has generated more than $1 billion in market capitalization value. He began teaching spiritual abundance courses at The Center for Spiritual Living in Fort Lauderdale, Florida, where he has served as a trustee for more than ten years. Through the Soul Currency Institute, he trains Soul Currency teachers, and coaches socially and environmentally responsible entrepreneurs and companies.

Chu has published dozens of articles on corporate finance and entrepreneurship in such publications as *The Wall Street Journal*, *Corporate Finance Week*, *MBA*, and *The Palm Beach Times*, and he has contributed to business anthologies on finance, venture capital, and entrepreneurship. His articles on abundance and personal wisdom now frequently appear on blogs and in a variety of personal growth and business magazines. Visit him at: **www.soulcurrency.com**.

Robert and Michelle Colt are cofounders of The Inside Game and Acting Success Now. Their process goes well beyond the many popularized approaches to success today. Their revolutionary method utilizes the most powerful tools and technologies on the planet today for your success and happiness. The result is you quickly learn to be, do, and have the creative success you choose.

Michelle's clarity and ability to ground you to the path of your success are phenomenal. She can pinpoint with great accuracy how you can quickly become unstuck and create the creative career you've always dreamed of. Her many successful clients include working actors and actresses, entrepreneurs, real estate developers, educators, doctors, and business and life coaches.

Robert knows how your mind works, as it relates to effortless, permanent self-motivation and superior performance, and how you can create lasting and successful creative results right now. Among his many successful clients are award-winning actors, writers, CEOs, CFOs, entrepreneurs, and business and life coaches.

Along with using the dynamic Acting Success Now Process and Sedona Method Coaching, the Colts both are certified master practitioners and coaches of neuro-linguistic programming, certified master practitioners of hypnosis, and members of the American Board of Neuro-Linguistic Programming and the American Board of Hypnotherapy.

Robert and Michelle split their time between New York City and Los Angeles. They may be contacted through the website: **www.actingsuccessnow.com.**

Janet Conner is a writer, columnist, teacher, and speaker with a simple but profound message: Everyone has direct and immediate access to the Voice of wisdom within. You just need to know how to activate it. Her book, *Writing Down Your Soul: How to Activate and Listen to the Extraordinary Voice Within* (Conari Press, January, 2009) has all the practical "how to" information you need to begin your own conversation.

After designing the first recruitment program at CNN and running a division of a search firm, Janet thought she was on track to have a lucrative consulting career. But then her marriage imploded and her career disintegrated. Out of desperation, she turned to Spirit on paper and demanded help. Janet quickly discovered that writing in a particular way brought her instant access to highly focused guidance and direction, as well as to breakthrough creativity and answers to her soul's deep questions.

Not content to have simply experienced the lifechanging power of writing, Janet set out to uncover the science that explains why writing by hand is the single most effective vehicle into the unconscious mind and beyond. Weaving together the most potent elements, Janet presents a simple, modern process in *Writing Down Your Soul* that anyone can use to access the wisdom that waits just below the conscious surface. With this practical tool at your disposal, you'll know exactly how to ask for and receive the guidance you need to live the life you want. Go to **www.writingdownyoursoul.com** to order the book, take classes, subscribe to the newsletter, participate in discussion boards, and much more.

Janet also created *Spiritual Geography*, the soul writing system that heals the broken heart. Take the interactive "Locator Quiz" at **www. spiritual geography.com** to determine your location. No matter where you are, there are workbooks and writing excersizes to help you move through the map to Peace.

You can also find Janet at **www. religionand spirituality.com**, where she's written a national column on practical spirituality since 2006.

John Darrouzet is a retired attorney, software engineer, and professional writer. He offers special counsel for leaders who make decisions in business, healthcare, higher education, and non-profit organizations, and for films in the entertainment industry. His up-to-date profile may be found on **www.linkedin.com**. If you are interested in making more creative decisions as a leader and would like to attend one of his programs, John may be reached by email at: **jldarrouzet@gmail.com**. Check out the entry "Do You Have a Method in Your Madness When Making Decisions?" on his blog: **http://special counselfordecisionmakers.blogspot.com**. As creator of The Decision-maker Process ™, please do not hesitate to contact John and take up a dialogue with him concerning any points he made in his essay "Creative Decision-making." He would love hearing from you.

Laura Duksta is an author, speaker, and entrepreneur. She is author of the best-selling book *I Love You More* (I Shine, 2003; Source-books, 2007)—over 200,000 sold—a book about love presented as a children's book. Its message is for every age and every season, as love transcends gender, age, race, and religion. Laura was featured in the 25th Year Anniversary issue of *Boca* magazine for making a difference in South Florida. *ILYM* was featured in *Pregnancy* magazine's coveted Buyers Guide. In 2003, it was voted Best Children's Book at the Do It Yourself Convention, where Laura's company, I Shine, also took home top honors for Best Publisher. Laura and *I Love You More* have been featured in dozens of publications locally and nationally: *USA Today*, *The Writer*, *Epregnancy*, The *Miami Herald*, The *Sun-Sentinel*, The *Patriot Ledger*, *The Palm Beach Post*. TV appearances include: NBC-6 in South Florida, "The Rick Sanchez Show," "Eye on Hilton Head," and "We the People."

As a speaker, Laura enjoys sharing her story with others, inspiring them to know that if she can do it, so can they. Laura has presented her program, "Self-Esteem through Love: Empowering our Children to Shine," to thousands of students, educators, and administrators nationwide. She speaks to women's groups, charitable foundations, and support groups, and shares how her biggest challenge, losing her hair, became her biggest blessing; and she speaks to aspiring authors about how she went from bartender to best-selling author. Laura has spoken for Learning Annex, National Alopecia Areata Foundation, Juvenile Diabetes Foundation, National Association of Women's Writers (Florida chapter), Gilda's Club, and Xango New School (a network marketing event), and she emceed the South Beach Wine and Food Festival Kidz Kitchen (with stars from The Food Network), as well as presenting school visits and author workshops. Laura lives in Ft. Lauderdale, Florida. Visit: **www.lauraduksta.com**.

David Ellzey has inspired nearly a quarter of a million people worldwide as a motivational speaker, seminar leader, actor, and coach. His work has been endorsed by Christiane Northrup, M.D., Norman Cousins, Susan Jeffers, Sally Jesse Rafael, and Robert

Mueller, former assistant undersecretary of the United Nations.

David's organization, David Ellzey Companies, LLC, runs training programs in the United States and Europe on life-changing personal growth techniques, including The Sedona Method. A former stage and screen actor, David's mastery is in blending sidesplitting humor with a unique and explosive message of how to remove emotional blocks to happiness and success. His clients include executives in leadership roles of global companies and Fortune 500 companies, small business entrepreneurs, and other people who are ready to finally transform and master their lives. David is a guest faculty member at The Omega Institute for Holistic Studies and T. Harv Eker's Peak Potentials.

David shared in receiving the prestigious Raoul Wallenburg Humanitarian Award as a member of the Big Apple Circus Clown Care℠ program for his work as a clown doctor in the innovative field of humor and healing in hospitals nationwide. The program, which was created by Michael Christiansen, celebrated its 20th year of service in 2006. For more information, phone 212-268-2500, or visit: **www.bigapplecircus.org.**

David is honored to have performed at The United Nations, Mother Theresa's orphanage in Agra, India, and The World Youth Festival in Moscow, where he received a standing ovation from an audience representing 160 nations for a performance supporting world peace.

David lives in New York City and can often be found near the edge of the Reservoir, his favorite spot in Central Park, enjoying the quiet of the water's reflections. To book him for speaking, coaching, or seminars, visit**: www.davidellzey.com**, send an email to: **david@davidellzey.com**, or phone: 212-996-5159.

Laura Faeth. Years ago, while trying her hand as a fashion model in New York City, Laura Faeth worked part-time at a health club, teaching nutrition and weight loss. Several co-workers turned her on to woo-woo icon Shirley MacLaine and her interest in spirituality took off like a bat out of hell. For over 15 years, Laura's dipped all of her toes, fingers, and especially her big head into a vast pool of metaphysics and alternative therapies. Everything from acupuncture to Reiki to using vowel sounds as mantras has been tested or studied by this modern day holistic junkie. Though a die-hard spiritual seeker, she's not your typical airy-fairy New Ager.

A summa cum laude graduate from the State University of New York at Oswego with a B.A. in communications and broadcasting, Laura was elected to the *Who's Who Among Students in American Universities and Colleges.* She spent over a decade working in radio research, advertising, and publishing before venturing into the wonderful, wacky world of writing.

Laura is still shocked that anyone actually thinks her writing isn't total dreck. When she received a letter from *Writer's Digest* indicating that her essay "The Healing Power of Rock 'n' Roll," was given an honorable mention (out of a total 19,000 entries) in their 76th Annual Writing Competition, she nearly went into anaphylactic shock. Then, her jaw hit the floor the day she found out that her spirited essay on the insanity of melding motherhood and writing would appear in the 2008 anthology *The Mom Egg*. Most amazingly of all, she can't believe her book, *I Found All the Parts: Healing the Soul through Rock 'n' Roll*, was published in 2008 by Wyatt-MacKenzie Publishing. Abraham Maslow would be proud. Visit: **www.soundofyoursoul.com**.

Howard Falco is a spiritual teacher and counselor (founder of **www.TruthSerum.net**) and financial advisor. Howie, as family and friends know him, grew up in the northwest suburbs of Chicago. After graduating high school in 1985, he attended Arizona State University, earning a bachelor's degree in business in 1989. Soon, he entered the financial world as a stockbroker/investment manager. He married in 1994 and has two children.

In August 2002, shortly after turning 35, he underwent a rapid, spontaneous expansion of consciousness. The shift in awareness took him completely by surprise and resulted in an immediate release from disharmony and fear. As far as he is concerned, his life could easily be described as ordinary until then. Identifying the event as a "peak experience," he says, "In an instant I realized the connection and oneness of everything in the world. Each object was revealed for its complete perfection. Peace pervaded every part of me."

Startled by what had happened, and having little prior knowledge of religion, spirituality, or quantum physics, Howie set out to research the phenomenon.

Four months later, a second, even more expansive peak experience took place, during which the core condition underlying human suffering was revealed to him. That condition is the inability to validate our existence through the experience of who we believe we are at any particular moment. Pursuing the depth of this insight unveiled answers to many of the larger questions that humanity asks on a regular basis, such as: "Who am I?" "Why am I here?" and "Why do I suffer?"

In order to understand the implications of these discoveries for his life and the lives of others, Howie spent the next three years exploring, embracing, and integrating his new understanding by keeping a record of his thoughts and by reading literature written throughout the ages from different disciplines. Ultimately, in 2006, he decided to set up a counseling practice and seminar business called Truth Serum, whose sole purpose is to deliver an important healing message to anyone ready and willing to embrace it: *We never are denied true peace if that is what we intend for our lives. We only have to realize that we are capable and worthy of the experience. This realization is what allows us to take the actions necessary to manifest it.*

Since that incredible period in his life, it has been Howie's desire to honor the information he learned by exposing it to others interested in achieving peace in their own lives. His daily intent is simply to offer what has been revealed to those who desire to know it. *I AM: The Power of Discovering Who You Really Are* is his first book.

Howie and his family currently live in Scottsdale, Arizona. He may be contacted at: **http://truthserum.net**.

Jeff Fasano is a photographer living his dream in New York City. He advocates: Find your passion and your truth that lies within and connect with it. Ever since he did this, it led him to living a life that he only imagined. For the past ten years, he has had the great fortune to meet and photograph notable artists from around the world and get paid for what he loves to do. He has created his life through his art, and it has opened doors to connect with musicians, actors, authors, designers, and all those who are creating their lives, their creative expression, and need to express it to the world. His talents and gifts as a photographer support them in doing this.

There is a soul-to-soul connection in Jeff's photo sessions. His images capture the essence of the person he's photographing and, through the images, that essence is revealed to the world. Along the way, he has worked with many artists who are living their dreams and giving their talents and gifts to the world: actors, such as Terrence Howard, James Earl Jones, Phylicia Rashad, Giancarlo Esposito, Morgan Freeman, Laurence Fishburn, Angela Bassett, and Taraji Henson; and musicians, such as Judy Collins, Quincy Jones, Jeff Tweedy of Wilco, Conor Oberst, Tommy Lee, David Johansen, Joseph Arthur, Cold War Kids, Nick Lowe, Graham Parker, James Galway, and Boyz II Men. The images they create together are used by these artists in many arenas and have assisted them in moving out further into the world. Record labels RCA,

Wildflower, Koch, and Decca among others, as well as magazines that include *Paste*, *Gotham*, *Vogue*, *InStyle*, *Elmore*, *Women Who Rock*, and *Guitar One* have published Jeff's images.

Jeff's passion has been the doorway into the life he now lives, and it has also led to other projects and endeavors, most notably the dream project of documenting the entire production of *Cat on a Hot Tin Roof* on Broadway in photos. That wonderful experience changed Jeff's life, as many others have as well, mainly due to the relationships he formed along the way. These relationships and accomplishments manifested simply because he listened to his heart when it asked him to find his passion. He found a vehicle for self-expression, a deep love for creating it, and thus has been able to receive what has appeared on his path because he made a commitment to his dream and himself. He is living that dream and believes you can, too.

Jeff may be reached through Jeff Fasano Photography, online at: **www.jefffasano.com**.

Eliana Gilad is an internationally recognized composer of healing music, a peace activist, an author, and founder of the Voices of Eden Healing Music and Peace Center in the Galilee, Israel. Her expertise is the conscious use of voice and rhythm as natural healing instruments, a practice that goes back to ancient matriarchal times. This natural healing has been scientifically demonstrated and medically researched in the neonatal ward of Meir Hospital, where physicians discovered that this form of music lowers blood pressure and heart rate.

Gilad is a frequent keynote presenter and performer at healing music, medical, and peace conferences throughout the world, including the Legends of Non-Violence Conference (2007), where she presented alongside Arun Gandhi (Mahatma Gandhi's grandson). She has also given concerts at the United Nations in New York, the UNESCO International Conference in Nazareth, Israel, and at the 2003 Thank Water Conference at the shores of the Sea of Galilee. Gilad is a passionate peace leader who brings people together and inspires them to action with such works as speaking for the Israeli-Palestinian Peace Conference, organizing a silent peace walk between Jewish and Arab villages in Israel based on Gandhi's principles, and hosting a standing-room only healing music event in honor of UN World Peace Day.

Her music has been recognized for providing a peaceful bridge between the Jewish and Arab populations of Israel as it bypasses spoken language and speaks to the heart. She also teaches Sacred Healing Music at the Voices of Eden Healing Music and Peace Center, a place where diverse groups and organizations also come to the Center to enjoy concerts, workshops, sacred peace tours, team-building retreats, and music meditations. Gilad has written two books and produced four musical albums and offers a free five-day stress release course based upon them available from her website: **www.voicesofeden.com**. She also leads multi-faith living peace tours in Israel—available through: **www.sacredpeacetours.com**. Gilad's music can be found at **www.cdbaby.com/all/music peace** and her inspirational writing at **www.inspirational**

message.blogspot.com and **www.voicesofeden.com/blog**, as well as in her free weekly newsletter "Inspirational Stories from the Holy Land."

"Rock Star Author" **Sandy Grason** is an international speaker and founder of the Journalution. She is the author of the bestselling book, *Journalution*, and the creator of the programs *Mastermind to Manifest: How to Use the Secrets of Manifesting to Create Unlimited Success* and *Secrets of Celebrity Endorsements: How to Get Fabulous Celebrity Endorsements for Your Book, Your Business and Your Products*. Sandy has addressed audiences for T. Harv Eker, Motorola, State Farm, and Royal Caribbean Cruise Lines. She is a faculty member at The Omega Institute. Sandy has been featured in *The Chicago Tribune, The Palm Beach Post, Body+Soul, Woman's Day, Balance,* and *Ocean Drive*. She has received glowing endorsements from celebrity-authors, such as Deepak Chopra, Debbie Ford, Mark Victor Hansen, John Gray, and Louise Hay.

As a coach, Sandy works with highly successful businesswomen and entrepreneurs who are in transition or ready for a major lifestyle performance upgrade. Sandy gives you permission to claim your magnificence, passionately, powerfully, and profitably. For more information on her products, events, and coaching programs, and to take Sandy's "Hot Mogul Quiz" and download a free audio chapter of *Journalution,* visit: **www.sandygrason.com**.

Kathi Handt and Jay Handt, D.C., are a husband and wife creative team. Ranked as one of the Top 10 Chiropractors in New York for 2006 and 2007 by the Consumer Research Council of America's *Guide to America's Top Chiropractors*, Dr. Jay Handt founded The New York Chiropractic Life Center for Health and Peak Performance in 1978 on the Upper West Side of Manhattan. He is a graduate of York College (CUNY) and The New York Chiropractic College, a diplomate of the National Board of Chiropractic Examiners, a member of the Board of Trustees of Life University, where he is also a President's Circle member and is on the board of directors of New Beginnings Seminars. He teaches on the post-graduate faculty of Life University, as well as at Palmer College of Chiropractic and Sherman College of Straight Chiropractic. He is a founding member of The New York Chiropractic Council and a member of the International Chiropractic Pediatric Association and the Florida Chiropractic Society.

Jay lectures on chiropractic care, personal growth, and motivation nationwide and creates programs for groups and businesses, depending on their needs. He presents Ropes course workshops to prospective students at Life University, allowing the participants to develop and focus on skills for achieving personal growth in all phases of life. Jay also presents fire walk programs to help people break free from their limitations, which he has been doing for almost 20 years!

Kathi Handt holds a bachelor's degree in music from Brooklyn College, and her creativity has expanded into everything she does. She has been a personal growth seminar leader, a motivational speaker, and a certified Ropes course facilitator. She is on the board of directors of New Beginnings Seminars. In partnership with Jay, and with Ruth and Dr. Chuck Ribley, Kathi taught and facilitated at the Inner Winners Seminars, a program that guided participants to move through limiting beliefs to reach their full potential. She currently lectures on leadership and teamwork for chiropractic students considering enrollment at Life University.

Kathi works closely with Jay on all of his programs, from creation to implementation. She is now in the research stages of finding ways to bring chiropractic to those in need all over the world, and has a special place in her heart for the children of the world. Kathi is also one of the founders and organizers of Business Success Team, a business networking group whose purpose is for its members to support each other with sound business tips and referrals. In addition to raising three children, she has worked as a real estate broker, travel agent, and life and health insurance broker.

Kathi and Jay are coauthors of a forthcoming book (New York Chiropractic Press, 2009) on healthy and successful living. Active in community service, together they donate their time and talents to ChiroMission, which delivers free chiropractic care to thousands in the Dominican Republic, to the Marine Corps' "Toys for Tots" program to help the needy, and to City Harvest food drives. It is their mission to help others constantly create excellence in their health and lives.

Visit the Handts online at: **www.newyorkchiropractic.com**.

Meg Haworth, Ph.D. healed over a dozen illnesses in her own body through understanding one thing: There is a huge difference between who we *think* we are and who we *know* we are. Today she assists others to tap into and live healthy, whole lives through connecting them with the vital essence of the soul. In her program *Earth School: Life Lessons from Your Soul*, Dr. Haworth teaches how to be a better student in the school of life through entering into a conscious partnership between the personality and the soul. She maintains that the soul is the only thing you cannot live without, so why not learn to live with its wisdom, healing, love, and guidance.

As a world-class intuitive healer and spiritual health expert, Dr. Haworth hosts her own radio show "Life Lessons from Your Soul." She is the author of a three-workbook series, which includes *Become Who You Are: The Stages of Spiritual Transformation* (Café Press, 2006), and is a contributing author to the anthology *Inspiration to Realization: Volume III* (Love Your Life Publishing, 2005).

Dr. Haworth offers a teleclass series on her workbooks, private telephone sessions, and individual in-person counseling sessions. She is a certified doctor of Ro-Hun Therapy, a process of enlightenment that is known as the most effective form of Transpersonal Psychotherapy available on the planet today. Additionally, Dr. Haworth is a professor at Barron University, an institution that offers masters and doctoral programs in integrative medicine through the University of California, Los Angeles. She lives in Los Angeles and is available to travel internationally to teach her spiritual development programs. Contact her through her website **www.doctormeg.com** or call for a free consultation: (323) 463-3636 or (626) 483-0214. Her archived radio shows are found at **www.bigmediausa.com**.

Rebecca Linder Hintze is an author, speaker, and emotional wellness therapist who has worked in private practice for more than a decade, completing thousands of private sessions. Her unique ability to reveal core belief patterns and facilitate the healing of dysfunctional family patterns has made her a leading expert on family issues.

A former broadcast journalist, she frequently lectures and leads workshops in cities throughout the United States on topics such as *"Strengthening Relationships," "Overcoming Self-Defeating Behavior," "Healing Destructive Family Patterns,"* and *"Creating Emotional Freedom."* She has worked in TV & radio in Salt Lake City, Utah, and Washington, D.C., and produced a one-hour PBS documentary series, *A Generation at Risk*.

In 2002, Rebecca published her first book, a healing workbook called *It's Time to Dance*, which sold out the first and second printing. Her second book, *Healing Your Family History*, with a foreword by Stephen R. Covey, was released by Hay House in October 2006. *Healing Your Family History,* now available in 13 countries and translated into 5 languages, is endorsed by several famed experts, including best-selling authors Christiane Northrop, M.D., James Jones, Ph.D., Stephen R. Covey, and international star Marie Osmond.

Rebecca is the co-founder (along with her own sisters Martha and Callie) of Pretty Sisters, an organization for women that was created specifically to help strengthen women and their families by building self-esteem, helping them enjoy life, and encouraging service. Pretty Sisters gather for various events across the United States and retail products made just for Pretty Sisters are available for sale online at **www.prettysisters.com**.

In 2002, Rebecca began publishing an online newsletter entitled, "Weekly Wisdom." Since that time, the newsletter has grown to include publication in various newsletters and newspapers around the world. The newsletter is a public service and may be reprinted and translated free of charge.

Rebecca is a graduate of Brigham Young University where she received several awards for outstanding achievement. She has pursued additional private course work in neural linguistic programming, rapid eye movement therapy, visual blueprint analysis, emotional release therapy, muscle response testing, and holistic health medicine.

Rebecca is a member of AMCAP (Association of Mormon Counselors and Psychotherapists). She is an active member of The Church of Jesus Christ of Latter-day Saints. She and her husband live in the Washington, D.C., area with their four children.

Carol Hoenig is a freelance writer and publishing consultant. Her novel *Without Grace* has received many awards and honors: silver medal for Book of the Year 2005 by *ForeWord* magazine, first place in fiction by the Do-It-Yourself Book Festival, and honorable mention from Jada Press and the New York Book Festival. Her book *The Author's Guide to Planning Book Events* was named a finalist by USA Book.

Carol's essays, articles, book reviews, and short stories have appeared in a wide number of publications. She blogs for *The Huffington Post* (**www.huffingtonpost.com/carol-hoenig**) and *Where I Stand* (**www.whereistand.com/Carol Hoenig**), covering politics, culture, the publishing industry, and the writing life. Carol also contributed to *Putting Your Passion into Print* by Arielle Eckstudt and David Henry Sterry (Workman, 2005). Arianna Huffington also invited Carol to contribute to *On Becoming Fearless* (Little, Brown, 2006). Tory Johnson, ABC's "Good Morning America" workplace contributor, invited Carol to submit an essay for her book *Will Work from Home* (Penguin, 2008). Her short story, *Snow Angels and Somersaults,* was a finalist for the 2007 Spring/Summer Glass Woman Prize, a bi-annual prize for women prose writers (**moondance.org/2007/winter/fiction/snow.html**).

Carol is on the board of directors of The Center for Independent Publishing in New York City. She is a member of the International Women's Writing Guild and the Women's National Book Association. For more information, visit: **www.carolhoenig.com.**

Dr. Beatrice Kraemer is a psychologist licensed to practice in New York State. Currently serving as Director of Career Services at The New School for Social Research, she holds a doctorate in human biology from the University of Ulm, Germany, a graduate degree in psychology from the University of Frankfurt, Germany, and a master's degree in environmental psychology from University of Surrey at Guildford, England.

For The New School, Dr. Kraemer teaches courses on eating disorders, environmental psychology, and psychological testing. She has taught clinical psychologists, medical doctors, and researchers in various departments at the University of Helsinki, Finland; The Robert-Fleuring-Institute, Netherlands; the University of Munich, Germany; the University of Berlin, Germany; and the University of Ulm. She held academic and scientific consulting appointments at the University of Frankfurt, Germany, and the Center for Psychotherapy Research in Stuttgart, Germany.

Dr. Kraemer has worked in the corporate sector, as well as in academic settings. She has run a consulting practice in Germany and New York City, through which she has trained and coached individuals and facilitated meetings for all levels of business. Her clients have included Exxon Chemical, Catalyst Strategies Group, Mypegasus, Institute for Training Seminars, Dekra GmbH, Media GmbH, and The New School for Social Research. Dr. Kraemer resides in New York City. To schedule a consultation or request a media interview, you may contact her by email at: **beatrice.kraemer@gmail.com**, or through her website: **www.beatricekraemer.com**.

Reverend Allan Lokos, an ordained Interfaith minister, is co-founder and Director of the Community of Peace and Spirituality in New York City (**www.interfaithhome.org**). He also has a private practice as a spiritual counselor working with individuals and couples and is writing a book about small, pocket practices as a way to inner peace in everyday life. Allan is a graduate of The New Seminary and has served as Dean of Students for The New Seminary and One Spirit Interfaith Seminary.

Allan has an active ministry performing weddings, baby blessings, and memorials. The range of wedding ceremonies he has created is enormous, from gala events marrying international celebrities to intimate celebrations on the terrace of his own home. (The most unusual of these may have been when he was invited to India to officiate a four-day wedding ceremony that culminated with the bride entering on an elephant.)

A student of Buddhadharma and a meditation teacher, Allan has been a member of Thich Nhat Hanh's Community of Mindfulness and has studied with several renowned meditation teachers, including his current mentor Sharon Salzberg. He regularly participates in meditation and study retreats.

Earlier in this life, Allan was a professional singer in opera and on Broadway, appearing in the original Broadway productions of *Oliver!, Pickwick,* and the Stratford Festival production of *The Pirates of Penzance.* He also performed the sacred music of Bach, Händel, Mozart, and Verdi, as well as hundreds of concerts throughout North America. He is a talented player of the Native American Flute and uses his musical background to compose flute music for meditations, chants, weddings, and funerals. He is also an accomplished photographer who combines his visual skills with his love of animals, and photographs wildlife from Central Park in New York to the plains and valleys of Eastern Africa.

Allan resides in New York City. He may be contacted by email at: **reval@earthlink.net**.

Mary Jane Mahan is an authentic living author and Chief Emotional Architect of Mary Jane Brain Productions. Her storytelling and practical teachings serve a mission to awaken hearts and illuminate minds to greater, bolder living through surrender, forgiveness, and courage. Mary Jane's writing style is intuitive, following the heart line of a story, like Nancy Drew. Her childhood gifts of acting and creative writing served her well while earning an English and communications degree from Villanova University and a master's degree in Speech Communication from the University of Georgia. With the guidance from her editor, Stephanie Gunning, Mary Jane birthed her first book *Love at the Pub* (2009), a historical account and modern day love affair with the Brick Store Pub in Decatur, Georgia, her adopted hometown (**www.loveatthepub.com**). Her passions are promoting peace, listening to John Coltrane, and playing rugby. Mary Jane loves to hear from like-minded souls at **www.maryjanebrain.com**.

Kim Marcille. An expert in strategic and transitional innovation, Kim teaches individuals and companies alike how to discover new possibilities for themselves and to amplify those possibilities into reality. Her email newsletter, "Possibility Tips," provides free resources and strategies for reframing issues and roadblocks, developing outrageous—yet implementable! —vision, and measuring the right things at the right time to accelerate success.

Kim brings her 25 years of corporate and entrepreneurial experience and her upbeat approach to every engagement. To find out more about her and to sign up for her newsletter, visit: **www.KimMarcille.com**.

Ann Moller is a singer, actress, and writer. She is delighted to be included in this anthology, having been involved in the worlds of creativity and personal growth throughout her life. As an actress and singer, she has received training at The Stella Adler School, The Barrow Group, and Ann Reinking's Broadway Theater Project, among others. Some of her favorite roles include Anya in *The Cherry Orchard,* Titania in *A Midsummer Night's Dream,* Rosa Bud in *The Mystery of Edwin Drood,* Maggie in *A Chorus Line,* and Agave in *The Bacchae*. In 2008, she played the ghost of a 1930's magician's assistant in the West Coast premiere of Rinne Groff's *Orange Lemon Egg Canary*. She can also be seen in a short film called *Is It Really Me?* which has won awards at film festivals around the world. She has worked and trained with such theater and film luminaries as Bartlett Sher, Ann Reinking, Gwen Verdon, Jeff Calhoun, Roy Scheider, and James Naughton. She is a graduate of Mama Gena's School of Womanly Arts and has received training in The Sedona Method and The Work of Byron Katie.

Ann grew up in Maine, holds a B.A. in English from Yale University, and is a proud member of The Actors' Equity Association. In addition to her theatrical work, she has been engaged to sing at classes, workshops, and private ceremonies and parties. For further information regarding her work as an actress and singer, please visit her at **www.annmoller.com**. To read more of her personal writing, please visit her blog at **www.butterflyscribe.blogspace.net**. Ann is also an experienced proofreader, editor, and writer, having worked on a freelance basis for such distinguished publishing companies as Random House, HarperCollins, and McCann Erickson Advertising, as well as for private clients. For further information about her work in this field, please go to **www.divaoftheword.com**.

Katherine Scott, creator of Voice of Destiny™, is a musical artist, composer, and coach who is on a mission to inspire and empower people in the areas of creativity and conscious living. Her musical performances and coaching programs help people connect to who they are. Through the lens of music and the human voice, she opens the way for them to appreciate and grow from their own valuable life experiences.

Katherine graduated with a bachelor of music degree from the University of Toronto and, as one of the founders and teachers of ProVoce Studios headed by Michael Warren of New York, she taught voice privately and also developed highly successful voice intensives. Before her move in 2006 to Vancouver, British Columbia, Canada, Katherine also taught seminars at Toronto's Learning Annex and appeared on CITY-TV's Breakfast Television. Her first CD, called *A Way of Knowing*, is a musical journey of change and renewal.

Katherine performs her well-received one-woman show "Seven Stories High: Songs and Stories in the Key of Life" at house concerts and other venues. The performance contains songs and stories about life and love, light and shadow, transformation and mystery, the hero's journey, and coming home. Song samples and a full CD are available at **www.voice ofdestinymusic.com**.

Katherine's five-week telecourse "Sounding Authentic" is designed to help coaches, speakers, and entrepreneurs free the complete power of their voice and improve their ability to connect to themselves and others. Voice of Destiny™ generously offers free voice tip subscriptions, which are available at **www.provoicetips.com** for singers and **www.powervoicetips.com** for the speaking voice.

Katherine is a member of the Positive Music Association, Harmonizing with Humanity, and Humanity Unites Brilliance (**www.voiceof destiny. hubhub.org**). These organizations help promote the genre of positive conscious music.

Contact Katherine at **www.katherine scott.com** for an overview of current offerings. For specific music-related information, visit **www.voiceof destinymusic.com**. To receive more sparks to ignite your creative fire, sign up for a free creativity course at **www.tickleyourmuse.com**.

Elaine Springer helps her clients achieve harmony between body, mind, emotions, and spirit by empowering them to live balanced lives. Through a combination of techniques and disciplines, she works with people to identify what is important to them, and helps them realize their intentions and achieve the balance that is necessary to perform well in life.

A certified Pilates instructor since 1988, Elaine studies and practices transcendental meditation, vibrational healing, and yoga. She experienced Ayurvedic medicine in Lancaster, Massachusetts, when Deepak Chopra was in residence there, and helped publicize his book *Quantum Healing*. She earned her certification as a Polarity Practitioner with the Ultrasonic Core Group in Malverne, New York, and as a Reiki Master Teacher with Robert Baker of Children of Light.

Elaine teaches the importance of bringing core values to daily endeavors so the world is a better place for everyone. She has worked with the American Cancer Society raising money and has counseled emotionally disturbed children. She brings grace, joy, and balance to everyone with whom she works.

Elaine's other professional experience includes owning Sunflowers Natural Food in Encinitas, California, assisting the director of a high-end French decorative arts gallery, and managing the private estate of German fashion designer Wolfgang Joop in New York City. While living in Hamburg, Germany, she managed the office of still life photographer Michael Somoroff.

She has a BA in Sociology and an MS in Education. She studied French literature and poetry at the L'lnstitut de Francais in Villefranche-sur-Mer, France, and completed her German studies at the Goethe Institute in Germany.

Elaine Springer is an active participant in the Questions and Answers segment on the professional networking website, LinkedIn. To view her contributions please go to: **www.linkedin.com/in/ebeautyandgrace**.

Elaine's website address is: **www.Ebeautyandgrace.com**. She would be thrilled and honored to hear all your thoughts and expressions. Call, write, sing, or send her a video. She would love to know who you are and accompany you on your journey.

Paige Stapleton is a writer, singer, and life explorer committed to self-inquiry and personal awareness. She is a principal of Stapleton Stark (**www.stapletonstark.com**), a business she created with her "St. Francis man," Brian Stark. Stapleton Stark provides creative and useful tools to help you explore, discover, and live your true desires. Paige and Brian are living their true desires through their workshops and ezine, *Authentic Living*. You can contact Paige by email at **info@stapletonstark.com**

Reverend Susanna Weiss is an ordained Interfaith minister and co-founder (with her husband, Rev. Allan Lokos) and director of the Community of Peace and Spirituality (**www.interfaithhome.org**). She studied at The New Seminary and is a graduate of One Spirit Interfaith Seminary.

Susanna performs all types of life cycle ceremonies, including weddings, baby blessings, and memorials, as well as performing hospital chaplaincy. She creates every wedding ceremony individually for the couple, and that ceremony is intended to reflect their unique vision, speaking to the heart in a meaningful, joyful, and spiritual way. Her background in languages is present in wedding ceremonies she has performed in French, German, and Spanish, and also those that have included elements in Chinese, Hebrew, Japanese, Korean, and Tagalog.

Susanna founded Personal Fitness Training, Inc. in 1980. Through this company she designs individualized programs for clients. She and her trainers specialize in working with physical issues that need a creative and extended approach. Susanna's 20-year career as a professional dancer and actress is reflected in her presentations of liturgical and sacred dance. She recently returned to professional dance, performing with Paradigm Dance Company at Symphony Space in New York City. She also studies flamenco.

Susanna enjoys early morning explorations of Central Park with the Artful Dodger, the irresistible golden retriever who shares Susanna and Allan's Upper West Side home. She also enjoys a daily meditation practice in the Buddhist tradition. You may contact Susanna by email at: **susannaweiss@earthlink.net**.

Maria Yraceburu is a gifted storyteller, sacred tablet dreamer, ceremonialist, and author of *Legends and Prophecies of the Quero Apache, Prayers and Meditations of the Quero Apache,* and *Wisdom of the Rainbow Serpent.* A Quero Apache diiyin and cross-cultural Earth teacher, she has experience in co-creating moments of ecstatic experience through energetic ritual. Her workshops and lectures involve, challenge, and transition participants with laughter and inspiration "to become all that we can be." Her native roots allow her a unique perspective on Taanaashkaada, the great Coming Together, a time steeped in Earth tradition and culture and a new understanding of conscious co-creation and passion. She is a go-between and guardian, a tour guide of Earth Wisdom. For more information, visit: **www.mariayraceburu.com**.

About the Editor

Stephanie Gunning, founder and publisher of Creative Blast Press, is an author, editor, and publishing consultant. Her A-list clientele includes bestselling authors (such as Gregg Braden, Hale Dwoskin, Ernest Chu, Sandy Grason, and Ruby Payne), major publishing firms (such as Hay House, McGraw-Hill, Crown, J.P. Tarcher, Health Communications, Perigee, and Jossey-Bass), top caliber literary agencies, and innovative small presses.

In addition to *Audacious Creativity*, Gunning has coauthored and ghostwritten 16 books, including *Whiff*, *Will Power*, *Easy Homeopathy*, *The Passion Principle*, *The American Institute of Homeopathy Handbook for Parents*, *Total Renewal*, *Exploring Feng Shui*, *Creating Home Sanctuaries with Feng Shui*, and *Creating Your Birth Plan*.

Gunning is the author of four audio programs on publishing, including: *Seven Quick & Easy Steps to Write and Sell Your First Book Proposal, Partner with Your Publisher, Social Media for Authors,* and *Planning Kick-Ass Book Events*. She is co-creator of the nine-week audio meditation course *Nine Steps to Heaven* and the popular online 30-day course *Stop Thinking Now*. She is the host of The Great American Think Out, an annual nationwide meditation event.

After graduating with a bachelors degree from Amherst College in 1984, Gunning launched her publishing career in New York City, rapidly rising through the editorial ranks at HarperCollins Publishers, then being recruited as a senior editor at Bantam

Doubleday Dell, and ultimately establishing her independent consulting practice, Stephanie Gunning Enterprises LLC, in 1996.

Currently she resides in Manhattan, where in addition to her writing, she teaches teleseminars and workshops, and consults on publishing options. To find out more about Ms. Gunning, and her products and services, visit: **www.stephaniegunning.com**.

Are You an Audacious Author?

Please contact Stephanie Gunning Enterprises for more information on our courses, programs, books, and audio programs on professional book publishing. We offer a variety of products and services designed to support accomplished and first-time authors.

Audacious Author Coaching

Being mentored in writing a book proposal or a manuscript, or in building a book-marketing platform is the quickest way to get the job done and ensure a successful outcome.

Write **contact@stephaniegunning.com** to get more details about our coaching programs. Space is limited, and therefore enrollment is by application.

Free Newsletter for Audacious Authors

To sign up for "The Publishing Insider News," our weekly online newsletter, and be notified about trends in publishing, upcoming courses, teleclasses and webinars, live events, and product releases, go to: **www.stephaniegunning.com**.

Free Tools for Audacious Authors

Get downloadable PDF articles and Mp3 audio recordings of Stephanie Gunning's interviews with experts on different aspects of publishing online at: **www.stephaniegunning.com/info/index.html**.

We look forward to hearing from you!

www.ingramcontent.com/pod-product-compliance
Lightning Source LLC
Chambersburg PA
CBHW071304110426
42743CB00042B/1169